Blue-Collar Blessed

Blue-Collar Blessed

A Humble Life in Idaho

Denny LaVé

Skyhorse Publishing

Skyhorse Publishing books may be purchased in bulk at special discounts for sales promotion, corporate gifts, fund-raising, or educational purposes. Special editions can also be created to specifications. For details, contact the Special Sales Department, Skyhorse Publishing, 307 West 36th Street, 11th Floor, New York, NY 10018 or info@skyhorsepublishing.com.

Skyhorse® and Skyhorse Publishing® are registered trademarks of Skyhorse Publishing, Inc.®, a Delaware corporation.

Visit our website at www.skyhorsepublishing.com.

10 9 8 7 6 5 4 3 2 1

Library of Congress Cataloging-in-Publication Data is available on file.

Cover design by David Ter-Avanesyan
Cover photo credit : Brendan M. LaVé, with Leica M10 75mm asph apo lens

ISBN: 978-1-5107-8592-2
Ebook ISBN: 978-1-5107-8617-2

Printed in the United States of America

To Fr. Brian Hawker, my friend. May you rest in peace.

CONTENTS

INTRODUCTION

The Call to Run

AMERICA IS one of the greatest countries in the world. It's one of the few places where someone from the lower class can grow to play a significant role in society and government. The opportunity is there, but the trap that prevents so many leaders from making a lasting impact is that they forget where they came from as they climb the ladder. Many lose their sense of humility, the trait that made them relatable and qualified for the job, if they ever had it in the first place.

Early in his career, some people considered Joe Biden one of those inspiring working-class figures who had risen through the government ranks and into a prominent role of service. By 2008, when he was elected the forty-sixth vice president of the United States, many felt that his values had changed.

At the time of the 2008 election, my wife, Gina, and I were renting a farmhouse outside Worley, Idaho, where we lived with our four young children and my wife's elderly aunt. There was a massive snowstorm that winter, and when it finally stopped, I put on my headphones and climbed onto the roof to shovel off the snow.

I was listening to a replay of a recent Joe Biden speech, but instead of an inspiring story, all I heard were partisan talking points.

Biden went to Catholic school growing up and regularly attends Mass, which would have imparted those moral values and principles to him, but much of what I heard contradicted the Catholic faith, specifically the abortion issue. The Democratic Party used to be the party of the workingman. That's who they once fought for, but this speech reflected none of that. The demographics were changing. *Wow, he's sold out. What happened?*

As he spoke, I thought, *If he can get to where he is today, so can I.* He came from a blue-collar family and is a normal human being. He isn't any more capable than me. And if I was blessed with the opportunity to serve, I wouldn't forget where I came from or the interests of the people I represented.

That's when I first had the inspiration to run for the US Senate.

My mentor, Donald Morgan, was advising me on business and life. He had briefly been involved in local politics, so I was hoping he could provide some perspective. As soon as I shared my idea to run, he said, "No, not now. It's not the right time. Just stay the course. Let your kids grow older. You don't want to do this when you have young children." He was adamant, and, looking back, he was right.

Also, from a financial standpoint, I was not prepared to launch a Senate campaign. Federal campaigns are expensive. One of the ways you get voters to take you seriously as a candidate is to put a big chunk of your own money into your campaign. If you don't have the money to invest, people won't learn who you are and what you stand for.

Running for Senate may not have been feasible at the time, but the idea stuck with me. I only told a few other people about my desire to run for office—friends, mentors, priests. I knew some thought I was off my rocker for even considering it, so I kept it close to the vest. Over the years, I checked in with Donald and he kept giving me the same answer. "Not yet. Wait for the right time."

I could have run for another office or a seat in local government, but I didn't have that calling. It never appealed to me. US senators serve six-year terms, which better positions them to make difficult choices, choices that are in the best interest of the country and their constituency. That's where I wanted to be, but I wasn't going to pursue it without the proper spiritual guidance, so I continued to pray about it. I wasn't looking for an answer, I was looking for a sign.

There is an old story about a man who is stuck on his rooftop during a flood and prays to God to save him. A man with a rowboat comes by, but the stranded man says, "No, I'm praying to God. He will come and save me." Soon after, a man with a motorboat comes by, and the stranded man gives him the same answer. He even told the man offering to rescue him in a helicopter the same thing. Sure enough, the water rose above the rooftop, and the stranded man drowned. When he reached heaven and came face-to-face with God, he asked, "I had faith; why didn't you save me?" God responded, "I sent you a rowboat, a motorboat, and a helicopter. What more do you want me to do?"

I believe God is subtle and acts through ordinary means. He puts people in your life and provides opportunities that you can capitalize on. It's not a direct push or an answer from above. What complicates this is that the voice of temptation is equally subtle and even more persuasive. When I was younger, I learned about discernment of spirits, which is the ability to determine whether your thoughts or ideas are coming from God or an evil spirit or are simply a product of basic human nature. There are a few heuristics, but the simplest is to discuss it with someone—a mentor or adviser—to ensure that you're acting in your best interest and not being misled. It's about being open and willing to take the guidance that's given to you, even when it's not the guidance you want to hear. I've learned that lesson the hard way many times, for when I act in a way that I believe God wants me to, things tend to work out for the best. When I don't or run away, things have gotten ugly.

Anticipating that I might run for the Senate in 2025, I handed over the day-to-day responsibilities of my business, a specialty construction company, in December 2024. If I decided to run, I didn't want to worry about the company at the last minute. That needed to be taken care of first. But I wasn't going to act without a sign.

Every morning, I perform a thirty-minute Christian meditation during which I pray and converse with God. There is a chair in the corner of my bedroom, with a picture of Our Lady of Guadalupe on one wall and a three-foot crucifix hanging directly in front of the chair on the wall opposite. I had gotten it ten years earlier because it reminded me of a crucifix I had seen in a thousand-year-old church on a mountaintop in the Pyrenees. And that's where I sit to do the morning meditation.

During that meditation, I often say, "God, if this is really what You want, and if this is really You speaking, then You need to make it crystal clear. I need someone to tell me it's time to take this step. And I need You to put me in connection with the right people, because I don't want to do this on my own. I need to know that this is coming from You and that it's not an ego trip."

In late December 2024, after two weeks of intense prayer, I attended church on Sunday. I was repeating that same prayer before and after Mass. I typically remain seated for ten minutes to steep in the experience before returning to everyday life. When I walked outside, it was freezing cold, thirty degrees. That's when one of my friends and mentors, John Green, approached me and asked, "Are you still thinking about this run for Senate?"

I had confided in John because he had been involved in politics while living in Texas and had been elected to the state legislature after moving to Idaho.

"Yes," I told him.

"Well, now's the time to do it. I'll connect you with some people. We'll get the northern part of the state locked up and then tackle the south."

That was my sign. I wasn't going to suffer the same fate as the man stranded during the flood. I was all in.

Since that day on my rooftop seventeen years earlier, America's politics had grown even more divisive, and the discourse had become increasingly ugly. Demonizing and attacking the opposing side became the go-to way for a politician to stir up support from their base, so it was viewed as the best path to reelection. Many politicians didn't have the people's best interests at heart. They were only interested in their quest for power.

There is a concept dating back to classical Greek philosophy that everyone has an idol they worship, something they put on a pedestal that becomes much more important to them than it should be. For some, it's pleasure—food, sex, or alcohol. Some worship money. Others want honor and esteem. And for a large swath of our political class, that idol is power. Rationally speaking, those who worship power are the least likely to use it responsibly. Their interests are self-serving, and they are more concerned with keeping power, for that is the idol they worship.

Power is not my idol. My idols are related to pleasure, and I continue to wage war against these false gods. I strive to put God first and possess both the awareness and humility to recognize my tendencies. Like Saint Paul, there's a thorn in my side. I've asked God to take it away, and He tells me His grace is sufficient, just like He told Paul. So, I continue to pursue what's right, not just what I desire, and humbly submit to God's plan for me.

For a long time, I was perfectly content to let others lead. I've since learned that those who don't want power are more likely to use it responsibly, either because they've been hurt by it in the past or understand the potential damage and unintended consequences of it. I don't want to leave society to those who would abuse that power, but unfortunately, given the current state of our politics, that seems to be the path we are on. There have been too many dirty deeds done dirt cheap, and few want to have an honest conversation about these problems. There is a current lack of effectiveness, leadership, and initiative. Government no longer promotes the common good, and so many people are upset today because they feel overlooked by our elected officials. That needs to change.

I've lived in Idaho since 2000. My wife was raised here, and we raised all our sons in this state, but that alone doesn't make for a good public servant. I understand the power of a strong community and have seen it lift up individuals in their time of need. I grew up in a dysfunctional family environment and witnessed the devastating effects that alcohol and substance abuse can have. I've dealt with and overcome various forms of trauma. I've seen the world through military eyes somewhat, having experienced ROTC and gone partway through the U.S. Marines Corps boot camp. I've lived in a religious house as well as a monastery in France. I understand what it's like to struggle to support a family and make ends meet. I've started a business and experienced many successes and failures along the way.

These difficult situations and life experiences have helped me understand that the issues facing Americans today are not black and white—people aren't defined by their political affiliation, and the other side of the aisle is not evil. We're all unique, beloved children of God. We're all human. Everyone has their good and bad qualities. Until we can all acknowledge this and begin to come together, partisan thinking and public discourse will be counterproductive and highly destructive. I believe there is a better way forward for us all, and it must start with humility, which drives my life.

I'm not talking about false humility or self-abnegation. I'm talking about genuine humility, which requires accepting both the good and the bad and acting in alignment with your values and what is true, not just what you want to be true. Writing this book has been the ultimate act of humility because I have had to face who I am and how I made myself that way, and I've chosen to reveal myself honestly and fully to you. Some of it's good, and some of it's painfully difficult to discuss, but it's all true. You deserve nothing less.

PART I

SEARCHING FOR HOME

CHAPTER 1

Constant Motion

I WAS only four years old when I left Billings, Montana, so I don't remember much. But I do remember that we lived in a two-story house on Canyon Drive with giant sunflowers in the backyard. I remember falling off a scooter, breaking my right collarbone, and having to color with my left hand. My older sister Shawn can verify that story—she has felt bad ever since because she thought I was being a "sissy" and made me walk home alone. I also remember receiving a glow-in-the-dark, paint-by-number kit about Han Solo from *The Empire Strikes Back* for my fourth birthday. What I don't remember is my father leaving my mother behind and secretly taking me and my sister across state lines to start another life.

My parents, Lou and Kathy, were married in 1971—one year before they graduated from high school in 1972. My sister was born in 1974, and I was born in 1976. My dad was an ironworker for his entire life. He was five foot eight but strong and stout. He was a masculine, physical guy who always portrayed himself as the dominant alpha. When we lived in Billings, he worked in a little town two hours away called Colstrip, Montana, where they were building a big coal-fired power plant. When that job ended, and there was no work locally, his next job took him out to California. Being an ironworker meant traveling to where the work was, so throughout my childhood, he would sometimes be away from home for months at a time.

On one of those trips back to visit us in Billings in 1980, my dad told my mom that he was taking Shawn and me on vacation, packed us into the car, and drove us to California with no intention of ever returning. My dad was twenty-eight, and he was having an affair with an eighteen-year-old woman in California named Maria. The impromptu trip to California was actually his attempt to get ahead of a custody battle. For the next six months, we didn't see or have any communication with our mom. Soon after that, they filed for divorce.

The four of us moved into a motel in Redwood City, California, right next to Ben Franklin's hot dog stand on El Camino Real. Then we moved to an apartment in the San Francisco Bay Area, in a town called Hayward, where I was enrolled in kindergarten at Hayward Lutheran Elementary School.

Maria's mom was half-Samoan and half-Chinese—her dad was of Irish descent but from Australia—so she resembled a Pacific Islander yet had an Irish temper. I don't recall the first time I met her or what happened. The whole trip was a blur. I do remember being confused about what to call her. "Are you 'Mom' now? Are you Maria?" We settled on "Ria," and that's how I referred to her throughout my childhood.

That first year had a much greater impact on my sister. Shawn, who was seven—only three years older than me—took care of us while we were together in California. She had finished second grade back in Billings. At the end of the school year, her teacher allowed the kids to take home any extra worksheets that were left over. So, Shawn brought this giant stack of worksheets with her to California, and she used those to teach me how to read. During that transitional period, she looked out for me as if I was her child.

I'm pretty sure what my father did would be a felony today,

but it wasn't back then. Both my sister and I had to meet with a court-ordered child psychologist for an evaluation as part of the divorce. Supposedly, in court, I said that I wanted to live with my father (that's what I was told, but I have no memory of this), so I stayed in California. My sister was sent back to Montana to live with my mother, who had remarried soon after the divorce.

According to the custody agreement, I would split my summer and Christmas vacations between parents. It was a twenty-hour car ride between Hayward and Billings, so I would fly as an unaccompanied minor, most often on Western Airlines. This was long before 9/11, so one parent could bring me right up to the boarding gate. After everyone else boarded the plane, the airline representative would hand me over to the gate agent, who would ensure I got safely on board and found my seat. Occasionally, if extra seats were available, I got bumped up to first class.

This arrangement worked well when we were younger, and it gave me a chance to see my sister. We were latchkey kids when we stayed at my mom's house. Mom worked as a receptionist and later as an office manager, so we were often left home alone. That's when Shawn became my mom all over again, and we did everything together back then.

After I moved to California, my relationship with my mom became strained. At first, I believe she was shell-shocked about the divorce and custody agreement. I know she argued with my father about not paying child support. (Today, the government has the right to step in when child support is not paid and deduct the amount from a paycheck, but this was not the case back in 1980.) As a result, there were times when I felt more like a pawn in a game between my parents.

My dad and Ria were married soon after the divorce was final. The apartment the three of us shared was small. They wanted a house, so when they finally found one with affordable rent, we moved across town to Erskine Lane by the Bay Bridge. It was a smaller house with a one-car garage. The kitchen was fitted with old yellow appliances and dark fake walnut cabinets. There was a giant lemon tree in the backyard, and it produced monster lemons, much bigger than the cute little lemons you see in the store. These were almost the size of grapefruits, and there were so many that we couldn't possibly use them all. Moving to a new home also meant a new school—Eden Garden Elementary. While we lived there for three years, until I was eight, my childhood was anything but stable.

My dad's mother was a widow who was broke and living alone in Billings with several cats. One day, he drove up there to bring her back to live with us in Hayward. After that, it wasn't long before my dad and Ria started having children of their own. Three years after I arrived in California, they gave birth to my sister. A year and a half later, Ria gave birth to another girl.

The house was getting crowded. I had one bedroom, my grandmother had another, and my parents were in the master with the two baby girls in cribs. They needed more room and decided it was time to buy their own house. California was getting too expensive, and my dad was an avid skier, so when I finished third grade in 1984, we picked up and moved to Ogden, Utah. We rented a house while they got on their feet and searched for a home to buy.

Moving to Utah was quite a shock to the system. Hayward had temperate weather, while Utah was in the high desert. It was extremely dry, which meant hot summers—some days reached over a hundred degrees—and very cold winters with a lot of powdery snow. But the weather wasn't the only factor that made the transition so difficult. I was also starting at a new school. It didn't help that when we arrived, my parents reenrolled me in the third grade because they couldn't remember what grade I was in. I was sitting in class thinking, "This all sounds very familiar." Eventually, it was sorted out, and I moved up to fourth grade, but I didn't remain in that school long.

Later that year, my parents purchased a home in nearby Uintah, Utah. It was significantly larger than our previous house, with a huge living room, a dining room, and a master bedroom. The house was set on two-thirds of an acre and had a barn in the back. The previous owner had put in a lot of work into the landscape, planting a couple of apple trees, apricot trees, lilies, and a gooseberry bush. Grapevines grew along the fence that separated the backyard from the garden behind the garage.

With the new home came another new school. I spent half of fourth grade at one school, and those of us in "lower" Uintah were sent to another school the next year. The most challenging part about switching schools was getting settled and finding new friends. Moving so much made me reserved, and I became hesitant to invest too much time in any one person or group because there was always the possibility that we would move and I would have to change schools again. Why put in the effort? I sought stability, and luckily, for a little while at least, I got a taste of it.

We remained at that house in Uintah until 1992, so I attended the same junior high for seventh, eighth, and ninth grade. That finally gave me the chance to settle in and find some friends. That period in Uintah was the most stable for me, and the town was a typical American suburb right on the fringe of the wilderness.

The town was so remote that my best friend Josh Moser and I spent most of our time in the woods, playing in the Weber River, and climbing dirt hillsides and cliffs. There was no convenience store in town—the closest store was three miles away. We grew up on the other side of the tracks, literally. If we ever wanted to buy something, we had to figure out a way to get across the river and the interstate on foot since the nearest bridge wasn't within walking distance. Once we did make it the store, we had to turn around and do it all over again to get back home. If my parents ever found out, I usually got in trouble, so it wasn't worth it. We didn't have to walk everywhere for long. When I got a little older, my father bought me a Yamaha Enduro dirt bike. Josh had a bike too, and together we rode those all over town.

As much as I liked being outside, I also loved computers and video games. When Vince Marcus moved to town in eighth grade, that's how we bonded. We quickly became friends and sometimes we'd break out the toy soldiers and spend half the day playing a tabletop war game called BattleTech. That appealed to the nerd side of my makeup.

Our family had a couple of horses at the house. Ria loved horses and was an experienced rider. She had rented a barn half a mile down the road from our house where she trained horses. I went riding a few times, but I wasn't skilled. One day, when I was twelve, right before I was supposed to leave to stay with my mother for the summer, Ria tried to teach me how to ride one of the younger horses she was training. Horses are very much attuned to the emotions of the rider, and this particular horse clearly sensed that I was uncomfortable. I wasn't in the saddle long before the horse bucked me off its back, and I smacked my face on the top rail of the corral. A few days later, I flew back to visit my mom with a big old shiner.

Utah was a very different state than California, with a very different culture. Today, the Mormon population in Utah is around 42 percent. Back in the 1980s, it was above 70 percent, and Uintah was no exception. There were significantly more Mormons than non-Mormons. Most youth sports and social activities were sponsored and organized by the Mormon church. Plays, fairs, and even troops of what was then called the Boy Scouts of America were affiliated with the church. A Mormon ward house—the building that serves as a chapel and gathering place for the congregation—was built right behind our home. That's where we'd go to play basketball and volleyball. Some of the Mormon kids didn't want to play with us non-Mormon kids. Not everyone was like that, but it created an "us versus them" environment, as there was some tension.

Ria also created some tension of her own in the community. She enjoyed sunbathing in a bikini in the backyard. She usually did this around the time when all the local dads were driving home from work. Many would stop to talk with her. That created a lot of jealous moms in the area.

During that period, my father was constantly on the road and spent long stints working in California. He'd be gone for three or four months at a time and would stay with Ria's parents, Desmond and Mitze, in San Carlos, a suburb south of San Francisco. While away, he might fly home briefly to visit, so most of our contact was over the phone. This was back when long-distance phone calls meant a roll of quarters at a pay phone. I might have talked to him once a week for five minutes on Sundays.

Our family continued to grow, and the house became increasingly crowded by the year, as my dad and Ria had four more children together while we lived in Uintah. I did a lot of babysitting during those days. Fortunately, the house was big, so my sisters shared a room, my brothers shared another, and since I was the oldest, I had my own room. That allowed me some privacy and, more importantly, time to read. I devoured books from an early age. I read so much that, after a while, Ria told me that I could only read for an hour a day. I also loved movies and playing video games, but she put a cap on that, too, to get me outside.

My dad and Ria ended up having nine children of their own—my youngest brother was twenty-three years younger than me. Add me and my sister to the mix, and my father had eleven children—six boys and five girls. I got along well with Ria. I love her, and she's a wonderful person, but I look back at that situation and think what a series of misguided choices she made. It was an impossible situation. She was only thirteen years older than me, so it's difficult to become a parent to so many children when you're barely an adult yourself.

My dad, on the other hand, had grown up amid chaos. His mom had seven kids with her first husband before he was killed in a bar fight. His dad had ten kids with his first wife before she died of tuberculosis. And that's how his parents first met—a widow and widower who got together to support each other. They ended up having two more kids together—my dad and my aunt—for a total of nineteen children between them.

There may have been a lot of mouths to feed in our house, but we were working class, and there was always food on the table. Every night, the family would all sit down for dinner. That was a big thing in our house, and it taught me that sitting down to share a meal together is crucial in strengthening the family bond. Because our basic needs were always met—food on the table and a roof over our heads—I never acknowledged the other issues that were going on with my parents and the impact they were having on the family.

When my dad was home, life wasn't great. My parents fought a lot, and my father had issues with drugs and alcohol. He struggled with substance abuse for as long as I can remember, and his job didn't help, because there is a lot you can get away with when living on the road. I'm sure that made things worse.

My siblings and I weren't always exposed to their arguing and fighting, but the friction between our parents was clear. There were several occasions when their relationship seemed to be over. When I finished the seventh grade, the whole family went to visit Dad in California, where he was staying with Grandpa Desmond and Grandma Mitze. He got into such a big fight with Ria that he and I spent the night outside, sleeping in the back of one of our pickup trucks. But no matter how bad the fight, they always got back together. It was a crazy environment and unhealthy for children, but it was all I knew, so it was normal for me.

While my dad and Ria had a volatile relationship and would frequently argue, there was never any violence or abuse in the home. I never witnessed any drug use. Despite his flaws, my dad was not a mean or vindictive person. He never deliberately tried to hurt me with his words. Even though he had his differences with my mom, and their relationship had ended in divorce, I never once heard him say a bad word about her. Rather, I sought his approval and wanted to be close with him. That's why, when he once told me that I was his best friend, I was on cloud nine. Then, the very next day, I heard him say the exact same thing to Ria. I was heartbroken. *We can't both be your best friend!* He wasn't self-aware enough to provide the emotional support we needed growing up. As I later came to realize, you can't expect someone to give you something they don't have.

The mood in the house may have been more contentious when my father was home, but it was a strange dichotomy because he was also fun to be around. He was always pranking me, and he loved a good joke. He was an early bird, so he would sneak into my room at six in the morning to pounce on me and wake me up. In the summer, he'd take us all for bike rides. In the winter, we'd go skiing or do what we called "hooky bobbing" after it snowed. That involved getting into an inner tube and hanging onto the rope tied to the back of the truck while my dad drove through town. The kids would all take turns riding the inner tubes—sometimes, the truck would drag two or three tubes at a time. *What could possibly go wrong?* The food at dinner was also much better when Dad was home. We got to eat a lot more steak compared to Ria's Stouffer's frozen potpies over rice. To be fair, we loved the frozen potpies, too!

A big turning point during my childhood occurred when I started playing Pop Warner football. At first, I wasn't sure if football was for me. Some of the kids who played were bigger than me, and I was a little intimidated. One day at practice, one of those kids tried to push me around. He picked a fight, but I didn't back down. We got into it right there on the field. I didn't win—I got clocked in the face with a helmet—but I stood my ground, and he never bothered me anymore. That gave me confidence. That's when I realized that I belonged on the team.

After making the junior high team in eighth grade, I wanted to play tight end. It sounded fun, and I thought I'd be good at it. I asked the coach, but he shot me down and told me, "You don't have the hands for that." (It wasn't a coincidence that one of the other coach's sons also wanted to play tight end.) That lit a fire inside me. *You don't think I have the hands? I'm going to have my hands on the ball every play.* Most kids with that mindset would go out for quarterback, but I wanted to be the center.

Nobody pays attention to the center. You get grouped in with the offensive line, which is where they usually stick the big kids who don't have the athleticism to play more skilled positions. But to me, the center was the unsung hero. Every single play started with the center. He was the first person with his hands on the ball. And if he didn't do his job—if he forgot the count, fumbled the snap, or didn't block—everything would go south. I wanted to prove I was up for that challenge.

The coach didn't believe that I was good enough to be a tight end. He tried to box me out, so I went out and showed him that I could be a pivotal part of the team, someone who touched the ball every single play. That fueled me like nothing before. And the more I played, the better I got. I wasn't athletic, and while I tried playing baseball and basketball, I could quickly tell that those sports weren't for me. But I started to shine when playing football, and it was all because of heart and drive. In ninth grade, I earned team MVP honors playing center—which is unheard of. No center is ever named MVP, especially in youth football.

To think, it all started as a way to prove myself. And that mindset drove me to some of my greatest successes and enjoyments in my life. I can acknowledge today that it also led to some of the biggest setbacks and challenges.

CHAPTER 2

The Catholic Awakening

I DON'T recall ever attending church while I lived in California. I led an agnostic life as a young kid. That all changed in the summer of 1988 when I was eleven years old. That's when I first met Father Gavin Bitzer, who lived with us for a week in Uintah.

I was baptized Lutheran as an infant because my dad was raised a Lutheran, but Ria was Catholic. After marrying my father, they would both become practicing Catholics. And not just run-of-the-mill Catholics—they were Traditional Latin Mass Catholics.

In the mid-1500s, following the Protestant Reformation, Pope Pius V standardized Catholic doctrine and the Mass for the entire Catholic Church. That remained intact until the 1960s, when a very radical shift occurred in the Church. Led by the Second Vatican Council (Vatican II), the Catholic Church created reforms that upended many of the rituals and formalities that had been tenets of the Catholic faith for hundreds of years. It involved allowing the Mass to be celebrated in other languages, including English. Those who were upset by the cultural changes and bending of tradition returned to the standardized Latin Mass as it had been before the Novus Ordo Mass was released after Vatican II.

Ria's father had attended a Christian Brothers school in

Australia when he was younger. This education formed him into a devout Catholic. When he witnessed the cultural upheaval within the Church in the 1960s and 1970s, he was conflicted. It was reflected in the Mass and also the mores of the faithful. It began with little things. Nuns and priests, who used to wear habits, were suddenly running around in jeans and T-shirts—as those old rules were no longer enforced. Then the priests and nuns began to leave their vocations en masse. The Church's stance on morality, family life, and social issues started to be widely ignored. Attendance at Mass widely declined. Many priests made outrageous claims that flew in the face of 1900 years of Church teaching. That's when Desmond gravitated toward the Latin Mass community.

Grandpa Desmond believed that faith was the greatest gift a person could have. The energy he had for the Church was contagious within our family. Suddenly, we all had more exposure to the faith. Without his deep and persevering devotion, I don't think my father or Ria would have become practicing Catholics.

After my parents moved to Uintah, they joined a tight-knit Latin Mass community of around fifty people. Since there wasn't a Latin Mass church in Utah, priests from the Society of Saint Pius X (SSPX) would frequently fly in from around the country—many from the Campbell and San Jose areas of California, others from Phoenix, Arizona—to stay with members of our community and celebrate the Latin Mass inside family homes. This was paid for by charitable contributions. The host family would pick up the visiting priest at the airport and put him up at their house for a week or more.

Father Gavin Bitzer was the first priest who stayed at our house. He was tall and clean-cut, with joyful eyes. At thirty-five years old, he was young but experienced. It takes about six years of training to become a priest, so the youngest are typically twenty-five years old. They tend to be placed in communities where they can grow and gain experience without too much responsibility. This allows them to mature into their role as a priest. So, by the time Father Bitzer came to stay with us, he was already well-respected.

The first thing I noticed about Father Bitzer was that he was down-to-earth. Too many priests and leaders can become so wrapped up in their roles and responsibilities that they forget it's okay to be human. Father Bitzer was fully human. He didn't constantly discuss God or religion; he was a normal guy who loved apple pie and ice cream.

We often went for walks together, venturing into the woods to go down by the river, where we made a competitive game out of stacking rocks on the shore. When I ran off to gather more rocks, he'd knock over my pile so he would always win. He was a priest who cheated! He was so relatable and fun to be around.

Sometimes, we just hung out. He never talked down to me but tried to meet me where I was and genuinely showed interest in what I was doing. Unlike my dad, who was always trying to prove himself and show how good he was, Father Bitzer was okay with who he was. There was never any agenda or ulterior motive, and that made time spent with him peaceful and calm. When in our home, he was a member of the family. But more than anything else, he set a good example and became a much-needed positive role model in my life.

The first Latin Mass I attended was in the spring of 1988 and it was unlike anything I had ever experienced. We kept the crucifix along with other religious statues and pictures on the Craftsman-style buffet table in our home, which we easily converted into a proper altar for Mass. With a few adjustments, our living room was suddenly transformed into a church for the twenty-five people seated within the cramped space.

When Father Bitzer and his altar server entered the room, the atmosphere shifted. I watched as they approached the altar and stood with their backs to the congregation as they spoke saying the initial prayers in Latin. I didn't speak Latin, but had a missal, a book that contains the prayers said or sung during Mass. One side of the page was in Latin, while the other side was in English. This made it easy to follow along.

The ritual's formality contrasted beautifully with the intimate setting. Scattered candles send a warm light throughout the room and the sound of bells hinted at a reverence that seemed to grow during the ceremony.

When Father Bitzer raised the host high above his head, followed by the chalice containing wine, everything the ceremony had been building toward peaked. This was the body and the blood being raised in succession—pure worship and the sense that God was truly present among us. Then, as if descending from that peak, the Mass moved into communion, where the divine came down to meet each of us personally.

The experience created a perfect circle of worship—one that made it impossible not to feel connected to something far greater than myself. A deep sense of worship, not in the evangelical sense, but that left me in awe and full of reverence for the inspiration God provided. It wasn't about holding hands and singing "Kumbaya." It was about worshipping the Lord, and it left a lasting impression on me the first time I experienced it. Never before had I felt that warm, comforting, and positive energy. To be in the presence of God was a transcendent reality.

I was suddenly a part of the oldest and "one true" religion.

People came from all over—including Salt Lake City, West Valley, and Ogden—to participate in the Latin Mass at our house. We were one of only three or four families that had the means and the space to host visiting priests, which we did frequently. Father Bitzer stayed with us four or five more times between 1988 and 1990. Other priests also visited and stayed at our home. The community scheduled the travel times and routes of the priests to ensure they weren't overburdened or burned out. During my early teenage years, I learned from many priests, but none of them had the same impact on me as Father Bitzer. That's where my relationship with God and the Church began.

Attending Latin Mass inside a family home was a unique way to experience the faith. It was a stark contrast between the enormous megachurches and the large-scale Masses that were becoming popular, and was more akin to the early days of the Church when it was an underground movement where Christians gathered to avoid persecution.

After a few years, we found other buildings and banquet halls to rent on a day-to-day basis to host Mass. Everyone would roll into the public venue and set up the altar, candles, vestments, chairs, and everything else required for Mass, then spend time together as a community before quickly breaking everything down afterward, to roll away until the next time.

Latin Mass was impactful for me because I chose to become a member of this community; I didn't grow up in it. If I had, perhaps I might have taken it for granted and not been as awestruck when I witnessed the ceremony and was welcomed into the community.

The result was that faith became a big part of our lives at home. We began praying the rosary every evening as a family. We would kneel in front of the altar that the visiting priests used to say Mass when in our home. Dad or Ria would start with a prayer, and each of the children would get their turn to lead a prayer.

When the Latin Mass wasn't available, or a priest wasn't in town, we'd go to Mass at Saint Jude's, the local Maronite Catholic church where many of those who attended the Latin Mass also went.

Becoming a member of the church community was an exhilarating experience. It felt like I had finally found a purpose—to love and serve God in this world and to be happy with Him in the next. That was why we were made, and that purpose gave me the direction and guidance for how to live my life. Instead of wandering, I had a target at which to aim. However, I soon realized that not everyone shared my feelings.

Later in the summer of 1988, my mother was in the process of leaving her psychotic second husband, Ron. He had a trailer on five acres across the street from Lake Elmo, on the north side of Billings. The plan was to meet my mom and Shawn in Missoula,

Montana. Then, together with my Uncle Dennis, we'd drive down to Savannah, Georgia, where she planned to live with her mom and grandmother for a while.

When I arrived in Missoula, the four of us piled into my mom's Mountain Dew–yellow Ford Maverick with a U-Haul cargo carrier on top. We made it to Savannah and stayed at the home of my great-grandmother, L. Vera Freeman. (The L stood for Lydia, but when she was a girl, "Lydia" was slang for an artificial birth control pill, so she went by her middle name. We just called her GG.) She was very tall and thin, always very well put together with her hair done up in a French twist. She'd go to the hairdresser every few weeks to have it redone.

Since I knew I wouldn't be able to attend church while I was away, I took my missal with me. The first Sunday we were at GG's, I took it out and was reading through my prayers when GG came over, and asked, "Oh honey, are you reading the Bible?"

"No, it's a missal," I said. I told her all about the Latin Mass and how I brought this with me to read through my prayers. "Do you want to take a look?" I asked.

"Oh no, your great-grandfather would roll over in his grave if he knew I had one of those."

I was confused. *Why would that be such a big deal? It was just a book.*

My great-grandmother was Christian; she would have loved it if I had been reading the Bible. Her side of our family were Freemasons and, as a member of the Order of the Eastern Star, she was opposed to Catholicism. There was genuine friction between her community and the Catholic community, one that had been ongoing for hundreds of years stemming from the influence the Church had over society. I didn't fully fathom it—I was too young—but that was the first time I saw how polarizing religion could be for people and how this was not a small thing. There was real meaning and consequence that came with this belief system and being a part of the community, but that didn't change what was in my heart.

My perspective on faith and what it meant to be a Catholic evolved from not having much of an opinion to becoming one of the most important commitments I could make and the highest calling. That's why, at twelve years old, I decided to convert to Catholicism, which meant being baptized.

First, I had to go through a brief catechism. It wasn't a formal Sunday school program, but I needed to show the priests that I had a basic understanding of the faith. That meant learning different prayers and being able to answer a series of questions before I could move forward. I would study on my own, and the priests who visited would be available to answer any of the questions I had. Overall, it took me a few months to memorize the required prayers and tenets of the faith, so it all happened quickly.

Father Bitzer was unavailable, so Father Albert Gonzalez traveled from Phoenix to perform the conditional baptism on a Sunday afternoon in September 1989 at the home of Bert and Jackie Gilbert, fellow members of the Latin Mass community who often hosted priests, just as we did. I was excited and had been looking forward to it. It was an intimate ceremony with only about twenty people, but it wasn't the ritual that stood out to me. What I remember most were the warm, white incandescent lights that lit up that old house. It made me feel comfortable and at peace, like I was finally in a place where I belonged.

Baptism wipes away all your sins to give you a fresh start moving forward. After being conditionally baptized, I confessed my sins to Father Gonzalez. I knew the basics and the obvious sins—lying, stealing, harming others, not honoring your parents—but at the time, I didn't yet have a strong grasp of what was and was not allowed according to the Catholic faith.

Aaron Swehla was a friend whose family also attended the Latin Mass. In the summer of 1990, when I was thirteen, the Swehla family told me about a church summer camp associated with Immaculate

Conception, a Latin Mass church located in Post Falls, Idaho. My parents agreed to let me go, and I rode up to Idaho with Aaron and his family. It was a long trip, with a lot of driving, but I was a veteran traveler by that point.

We met everyone at the church in Post Falls and then boarded a bus for the four-hour trip to Glacier National Park in Montana, where we would spend two weeks at summer camp. Although it was primarily a church camp, we made the most of visiting the nearby national park, hiking and playing in the river.

I was a shy kid, and while I enjoyed camp, I didn't go out of my way to make friends with any of the other kids. While they liked camp and playing outside, it was the church component that drew me. I rarely discussed God or my faith, even back home in Utah. But I was comfortable talking with the seminarians—and their lives fascinated me.

After summer camp ended, I didn't want to go home. The priests so intrigued me that I wanted to see how they lived. So I asked one of the priests if I could return with them to Immaculate Conception for another week. The priest agreed and I called my parents; they were okay with it, too. When we returned to Post Falls and all the other campers left, I settled into the priory, where I would sleep on the living room floor for the next week—something you could only get away with back in the 1980s.

Immaculate Conception was a very simple Western American church. They had a school with a small church building on top. The priory was a tiny, brick-clad house and inside the church were stained-glass windows that had been repurposed from another church that was being demolished.

Father John Rizzo was the priest in charge of Immaculate Conception. Much like Father Bitzer, he was also thirty-five years old with a simple humanity that intrigued me. During my week's stay, Father Rizzo drove me and two older teenagers around town. There he was, with his black robe and white Roman collar, trying to make inroads with these two older kids who seemed more interested in blasting music on the radio than in what he had to say. I don't know if he was successful at getting through to them, but I could see that he was willing to try. He didn't shame or judge them; he was just there, living in their world and trying to relate.

Most of the priests I have met are good men. A few priests have left me scratching my head, but they are generous and loving men who want to do good in the world. They care about others and want people to thrive spiritually. That's why, at the time, I viewed both Father Bitzer and Father Rizzo with such reverence. Life at home was chaotic and volatile. My father was gone for months at a time. Finally, here were two positive male role models I could look up to—something that had been missing in my young life.

My week at Immaculate Conception was a positive experience. When it was over, I boarded a Greyhound bus by myself and made the long journey back home to Utah. I had a lot to think about on that bus ride. The camp, or more specifically my week spent living at the priory, further solidified my interest in the Church. I started to think seriously about the religious life, even joining the priesthood when I got older, but inside I was conflicted—not with my faith. That euphoria I initially felt after converting to Catholicism soon turned into a struggle as I started to feel like I wasn't living up to the person the Church wanted me to be. I began waging a war within, one I would continue to fight for most of my adult life.

Kids are the same everywhere. When we're young, we're curious, even a bit mischievous. We're told not to do things, that certain things are bad for us or forbidden, and that only makes us want to do them more. It's innocent and we outgrow it. But it becomes a problem when our desires and impulses run deep, influenced by our early developmental upbringing.

Like any small town, the grade-school kids in my Uintah neighborhood shared pornography—dirty magazines or adult videos. It was out there. It was talked about and shared, but I never spoke to my friends about the feelings I experienced. I didn't talk openly about the impure thoughts and urges that resulted in feeling overwhelming shame. I knew that looking at pornography was forbidden by the Church, so I would tell the priests during confession if I had looked at it. None of them ever passed judgment or said anything to make me feel worse. I could do that all by myself.

A pattern soon developed. First, I'd chastise myself up for succumbing to these urges and temptations. Then, I'd be thankful that God was forgiving, and I'd promise myself that I would never do this again. I would be better. But then the urge would bubble up inside me, and I would succumb again to temptation. Sometimes, after I fell and sinned, I figured I might as well get my money's worth until confession. In for a penny, in for a pound. But that would only result in a heavier weight on my conscience. No matter how badly I wanted to do better next time, it was a vicious cycle that always repeated.

Looking back at the situation today, I can see that the attitude I had and the way I approached it was similar to that of an addict. Any addict knows that you can't white-knuckle your way through recovery by willpower alone and hope to succeed. But that's the approach I took to overcome what I believed at the time to be a very significant character flaw—and a sin. This was reinforced by the Church's teachings. Many priests believe our sexuality is something that is under full control of our rational selves. They view the inability to control sexual drive as a character defect.

In the Church there tends to be a lot of focus on what you can and can't do, so it's easy to mischaracterize the Church as a guilt factory. And because I spent a lot of time doing the things I was told not to do, I felt like I was going to confession all the time. The environment I grew up in put a premium on fast confessions because of the limited amount of time the priests were in town. If sins are like weeds, the confessor would lop them off at the ground. The problem was that they could never get to the root, and that led to many negative self-beliefs.

I continuously felt that what I was thinking and feeling was wrong—that it was a sin and evil. In my teenage mind, I was weak and not trying hard enough. That evolved into thinking I was the problem and a bad person. *Why can't I get past this?* That's challenging to live through, and it can wreak havoc on your psyche. And it's how I ended up in some dark places. Many Catholics arrive at this point, which is not what the Church teaches and that's sad. I've since learned that something much bigger was going on with me. I grew up thinking I was responsible for my actions. We all like to think we're in control, but our brains don't always allow that.

Research has determined that exposure to pornography and hyper-sexualization at an early age can impact brain development. This can lead to numerous social and mental health issues, including impulse control, anxiety, depression, and addiction. Today there is little question that early exposure to pornography causes serious problems.

My exposure to pornography started when I was three years old after stumbling upon an adult magazine in my dad's room. (I also vaguely recall seeing two people have sex. I can't be certain, but every indication suggests one of them was my father.) He never intentionally exposed me to pornography; he was just careless. When we moved to the house in Hayward, I quickly learned that the pay-per-view pornography channels on TV were viewable at certain hours of the night, so I started watching those. There I was, five or six years old, and instead of watching cartoons, I was watching pornography. Soon, I was stashing nude pictures in my room. When Ria found them, she freaked out and I'd get in trouble.

Years later, I would realize that early exposure to pornography impacted my brain chemistry so that it became a coping mechanism for feelings of worthlessness as I grew older. Once it got its hooks in me, I started looking for it everywhere. I wasn't consciously seeking arousal; it was more a conditioned response to feeling lonely and afraid. Some people cope by eating, and others turn to alcohol and drugs. Some people cope through sex, whether real-life experiences or imagination. That became problematic, especially once I became a Catholic. I may have had a purpose—to know, love, and serve God—which gave me a target to shoot at, but it felt like I was always missing it by about one or two degrees. That led to me constantly having to correct my course to get back on target. But I didn't understand the root cause of the issue, so I never received the proper guidance.

I recently listened to Father Sean Kilcawley, from the Diocese of Lincoln, Nebraska, give a presentation to a group of young adults about this topic. He told the story of how a couple reached out to him after they caught their twelve-year-old son looking at pornography on the computer. The three of them came in for a meeting, and it was immediately clear that the parents were shocked, angry, and embarrassed about what had happened.

Calmly, Father Kilcawley pulled the boy aside and asked him, "If Jesus walked into the room and saw you looking at those pictures, what do you think He would say?"

"He'd be angry and upset," the boy said. "He'd probably tell me I was going to hell."

Father Kilcawley looked at him and told him, "No. That's not what He would say at all. He'd tell you that an enemy had done this to you and that He's sorry it has happened. He'd say 'I love you, and I'm going to do everything in my power to make it better.' He'd keep repeating that same message over and over until you believed it." When I heard this, I broke down and cried.

Nobody ever wants to get stuck in the pit, but it happens to all of us for various reasons. We beat ourselves up, or think of ourselves as being gross, a disgusting mess. That's not how God sees us. What He sees is someone who has been wronged and needs help and love. Shame is a self-perpetuating cycle, and being able to recognize when it occurs creates space to understand that *you are not your actions*. I have battled this most of my adult life. And it wasn't until recently that I was finally able to free myself from that internal battle.

Today, I can say to myself, "I'm sorry that happened to you. You should have been treated better by your family and society because you deserve better. I want to do everything I can to help you get better." But I didn't have that perspective as a child. Very few children do, which is why so many kids today are suffering for reasons that aren't their fault. Shame only prevents them from speaking up and getting the help they need, so the problem festers unaddressed. It's only by talking about it that kids can better understand the root cause of their issues. A parent's job is to create an environment where children feel safe to openly talk about their struggles. It's not something that happens overnight; it's a process and one that doesn't require perfection.

What I love about the Church is that you're not expected to make a linear progression, you're not expected to be perfect. You can embrace God and the faith and still make mistakes. God forgives and shows us grace so that we can recover and try again. The journey of faith is one marked by ups and downs, peaks and valleys. It's what keeps us humble and striving toward our true potential.

CHAPTER 3

Structure within Chaos

APART FROM my faith, very little in my life remained consistent for long. The stability I had found in Uintah after living there for eight years ended abruptly in 1993, during the Christmas break of my sophomore year of high school.

After assessing and analyzing their financial situation, my parents decided to sell our home. We were now a large family, and we needed a much bigger house. This time, instead of buying a house, they would build their own. It would be less expensive and it would provide them with more space for the horses, plus they could add a garden on the property.

However, there was a problem. My dad had been injured and was out of work, so money was tight. We couldn't purchase the land right away. After our house sold in the winter of 1993, we needed a place to stay while my parents got back on their feet and searched for an affordable plot of land.

Grandpa Desmond and Grandma Mitze invited us into their home in San Carlos, California. We knew it would be cramped, but that was where we went. I didn't want to pick up and move again, but there was nothing I could do about it. The nine of us packed into our big Chevy pickup with an extended cab and a canopy on the back for the thirteen-hour drive to the coast. I had just turned sixteen; my sisters were eight, seven, and five, and my brothers were only three and one. Getting us all into the back cab was a tight squeeze, but we made the most of the space. There was a carpet kit on the bed and a sliding rear window, so the younger kids could hang out in the cab and crawl back and forth between the front and back of the truck.

I had been to my grandparents' house before; it was the same house where my dad stayed when on the road and working in California. So it wasn't new, but it was small: Eleven people living in a nine-hundred-square-foot, three-bedroom, one-bath house. I did not have my own room here but shared a room with my three-year-old brother. My parents slept in a hideaway bed in the living room. I knew it was temporary; the plan was always to return to Utah; I just didn't know how long that would take.

The first challenge was finding another new school—this time, high school. I needed to figure out which schools had classes that were still available and would fit with the class load that I started with back in Utah. I soon enrolled in Carlmont High School in Belmont, California. It was a brand-new environment that I wasn't remotely prepared for.

Belmont was a wealthy, upper-class neighborhood, predominately white and Asian. Half of the students were bused in from East Palo Alto, so there were also many African American, Hispanic, and Pacific Islander students. There was a significant gang presence at the school, which led to a lot of violence—a far cry from peaceful Uintah, where security consisted of the sole principal. At Carlmont, we had real security officers. The school had done away with lockers because it made it too easy for students to store weapons and drugs.

After six months of living in California, my parents finally bought a plot of land in North Ogden, Utah, slightly north of where we previously lived in Uintah. With the land secured, they hired a contractor to begin building and would occasionally fly back home to oversee construction, which was expected to take a year. Meanwhile, I was starting my junior year of high school. So for the entire school year in California, I knew I would not be there for my senior year. I had no reason to get attached to the school or the community.

What I wanted more than anything was a car, and nobody was going to give me one. That meant that I had to go out and find a job. I was hired as a bagger at a little family-owned grocery store called Foodville. That's where I got my first taste of how unions operate. A temporary employee could be hired for a ninety-day probationary period before they had to join the union. Once they were part of the union, the company had to pay union wages. As I approached the end of my probationary period, my manager told me, "Hey, we don't need you anymore." They got rid of me, so they didn't have to pay the benefits. That was a good lesson: I learned about the "company first" attitude in the professional world, and it's one reason why I get upset when I see big companies that don't take care of their rank-and-file employees.

I wasn't unemployed long. After I was let go at Foodville, I walked next door and got a job at the local bakery, which was a different but equally crazy environment. There were some young employees from East Palo Alto with gang affiliations, and I'd hear stories about fights and the crazy happenings going on in their community. It made home life feel tame in comparison.

At the time, I was just waiting to return to Utah and pick up my old life. However, I learned something about myself in the process—a trait that would become my superpower for the rest of that year. I discovered that I thrived when I had more responsibility. When football season started, I kept the job. That meant my days were packed with school, practice, and work, with hardly any time in between to do anything else. Some kids might have felt overwhelmed by this, but I was the opposite. I excelled in that environment. It turns out that I needed that structured discipline to function at my best and reach my full potential.

When I set my mind to doing something, I always follow through. It's not that failure wasn't an option; I simply didn't consider it. I just kept working until I achieved my goal. That's how I approached school and sports, and that year, it's how I approached making enough money to buy a car.

I bought a silver 1985 Honda Accord that was in decent condition. It was great having a car! It would have been even better if I could have driven it. But I couldn't afford the auto insurance, so I wasn't allowed to drive it in California. It just sat in the driveway. After working all summer, I was still forced to pedal the old ten-speed bike my father had owned since he was a young man.

The first time I drove that car was when I packed it up in the summer of 1994 with all my belongings and returned to Utah.

Our new house in North Ogden was big, with a tiled front entry with peach-colored grout. There was a large formal living area and an ample family room with a pool table and an entertainment area for watching movies, plus a spacious kitchen with vaulted ceilings. There was so much light! With the high ceilings and big picture windows, a tremendous amount of natural light flooded into the house.

I enjoyed having my own money in California, and I wanted to keep working. Once we had settled in, I took a job at Fred Meyer, a popular supermarket chain in the Pacific Northwest. It was June, so school wasn't going to start for a couple of months. I worked about forty hours a week sweeping floors, stocking shelves, bagging groceries, and chasing down carts in the parking lot. I worked enough hours to be eligible for health insurance. Since I already had health insurance through my dad's employer, I was able to opt out of the program and convert the portion of my paycheck typically allocated for insurance into cash. That gave me a little extra pocket money each week to spend while out with my friends.

I disliked the dominance rituals that occurred within many male friend groups. They'd fight over who was the alpha, but I never cared about that. *If you want to be the alpha, fine. It doesn't matter to me.* That attitude only made kids upset because whoever wanted to be the alpha then had to prove it. That's why I was more of a lone wolf, existing on the social fringe. That doesn't mean that I was an outsider. By the time I reached high school, I had learned how to adapt to different environments and to do what I needed to do to fit in with various groups. It was like putting on a different uniform, and while I got along with many people, I was never a part of any one group.

I was still friendly with Vince Marcus (my friend whom I played video games with), and we started hanging out more when I returned to Utah that summer. It was through his group of friends that I met Beth and we started dating. She didn't go to Bonneville High School, but attended Morgan High School up Weber Canyon. Years later, I learned that Vince had liked her and was trying to start a relationship with her when I returned to town from California. I had no idea that he had eyes for her, or I wouldn't have gone out with her.

Beth wasn't my first girlfriend (I had dated another Beth back in California), but this relationship progressed faster than any I had in the past. After one date, I took her home and she suggested sneaking into the small travel trailer her parents had parked in their driveway. We weren't there very long before there was a knock on the door. It was her father, and he wasn't happy. It could have been a lot worse—he could have been the angry shotgun-wielding type—but he just told me to go home and that we'd deal with it later.

The next day I was at work when I got a call from Ria asking me why Beth's father wanted to have a conversation. "Before I talk with him," she told me. "I want to talk with you when you get home tonight." I already knew this wasn't going to end well and dreaded returning home.

Luckily, when I got home my parents weren't there. What I did next surprised even me, and to this day, I still have no idea why I did it, but I took a pair of hair clippers, went into the bathroom, and buzzed off all my hair. I felt guilty and ashamed, like I was preparing to go to prison, and when you get to prison, they shave your hair. This was a way to punish myself for messing up again, not living up to the type of person my parents and the Church wanted me to be. The person I wanted to be. The buzz cut became a physical manifestation of my shame.

My dad came home first. He didn't comment on the new haircut, just said, "Come outside. Let's talk."

I sucked it up and followed him outside. Once we were away from my brothers and sisters, he asked, "What's going on? And shoot straight with me."

This would be a painfully awkward conversation. I didn't want to tell him what had happened. But I knew it was going to get out anyway and I didn't have a choice. I told him everything. When I got to the end of the story, he took a deep breath, rolled his eyes, and said, "You might want to consider lying to Ria about this."

This was the dumbest advice I'd ever received from my dad. "Wow! Really? That's your advice? Ria has known me since I was four, and every time I lied to her, she saw right through me."

It was true. I never lied to Ria about anything big. It was little things like "I didn't eat the cookies" or "I didn't go to that place you told me not to go." It didn't matter what it was; she could always tell when I was lying, and I wasn't going to lie to her again.

When Ria got home and sat me down for the dreaded talk, I told her the truth. The verdict: I was grounded for a month. How embarrassing. I was going to be a senior in high school and I was grounded for a month. Beth was grounded, too. Her Mormon family was against fooling around, so we were forbidden from seeing each other. That pretty much ended our relationship.

I looked forward to returning to my old high school in the fall. Bonneville was a good school, and I felt comfortable there. Our house in North Ogden was nine miles away from school, so it was a bit outside the Bonneville HS jurisdiction. Strictly speaking, I don't think I was supposed to attend the same school. I'm not sure if my parents had to do any wrangling, but when I let the administration know that I was back in town and wanted to reenroll, they didn't give me any trouble. Either way, it was one of the rare, seamless transitions from school to school that I had experienced. I already knew most of the kids and teachers. I had a pretty good understanding of the curriculum and what was expected of me academically. I picked right back up where I left off.

When football season began at the end of the summer, I kept my job working nights at Fred Meyer so I could continue earning money. Just like back in California, my days were packed. I woke up, drove to school, went to practice, drove to work, and by the time I returned home, it was almost midnight. I was rarely at home most of my senior year, which meant I'd do homework early in the morning, in between classes, or in the rare free time between school, football, and work. My schoolwork didn't suffer. I was enrolled in AP classes and still managed to get very good grades. The AP exams at the end of the year could also earn me college credit. That got me thinking about my future and what I wanted to do after graduation.

Before we had left Utah a year and a half earlier, the Latin Mass had started to transition from being held in family homes to being hosted in formal event spaces on a transient basis. When we returned, this was more common as the community had grown. Where once we used to have twenty or thirty people attending Mass inside a home, now we could accommodate seventy or eighty people in one of the larger spaces. Those in charge of the community and the event arrangements showed a great deal of devotion, as managing and relocating all the equipment and gear was not easy.

We continued to fly visiting priests into the area to stay with community members, and to host them in our homes when needed. Father Teague had stayed with us around that time, and it was during one of his visits to our home that I walked into the bathroom to find the liner notes of my *They Might Be Giants* album sitting on the back of the toilet. I listened to *They Might Be Giants* in high school, and I owned a couple of their albums. That was now Father Teague's bathroom reading. After going over all the lyrics to see if they aligned with Catholic values, he wasn't impressed and had a talk with me about my taste in music. I felt the lyrics were mostly harmless, but he believed something different.

I was still considering the priesthood, so when Father Teague stayed with us, I talked to him about it. He listened and then, without providing much explanation, said, "I don't think you would be a good fit for the priesthood." He didn't give me a reason, but I have some ideas.

I don't believe *They Might Be Giants* can be blamed for Father Teague recommending I not become a priest. If I were to guess, I think his reluctance had more to do with the crazy situation at home. Many priests believe that growing up in a dysfunctional environment can have consequences for children when they become adults. When people don't understand how to address these issues, one strategy is to sometimes avoid the problem rather than deal with it. That's conjecture, but it wouldn't be the last time someone in the Church gave me a similar message without explanation.

If it were any other situation, I might have taken the priest's dismissal as a challenge, just as I did when playing junior high football, but that's not how I reacted. My faith and devotion never wavered, but I struggled and was confused because my priorities were conflicted. On one hand, I liked hanging out with my friends and chasing girls. On the other hand, I was supposed to live according to the Evangelical Counsels (poverty, chastity, and obedience) to be in alignment with God, only to be told that path wasn't right for me. Throughout it all, I felt ashamed, which made me wonder if I was unworthy of the path I sought with the Church. Father Teague's response was unexpected and disappointing. It felt like God had a plan for me, and that plan was not materializing.

I began to question God's motives. If God was all-powerful, why should He create obstacles to prevent me from doing what He wanted me to do? Is He all-powerful or not? If He is, then let's figure out a way to do what He wants me to do. And if He's not, which doesn't seem to be possible, then there is a disconnect between what I hear in church and what I see happening in the real world.

My inability to live up to what I believed was God's standard and to follow His plan created a lot of inner turmoil. Maybe I would have been better off had I not been a Catholic, because then I wouldn't have been so hard on myself. I might not think I was doing anything wrong, and that would have been a much easier way to live. After all, ignorance can be bliss. But I saw it differently and understood the tremendous benefits, even then.

Not many people have a clear sense of purpose. They follow their passions and their idols only to reach their mid-forties and realize they're miserable and their life is a train wreck. They've pursued money and pleasure, even gotten everything they thought they wanted, yet still feel empty and unfulfilled. Maybe they take an honest look at their lives and feel that something is missing.

As a Catholic, you realize that the Creator of the universe loves you. You are one of His children, and He's asking you to follow the guidelines He has set forth so that you can spend an eternity with Him in heaven. But that doesn't mean there won't be any suffering in this world. We all suffer. We all endure hardship. No religion will exempt you from that. But if you're going to face those challenges, wouldn't it be nice to know where you're headed when this life is over so that we have a perspective that better allows us to persevere?

Now that entering the priesthood was off the table, I shifted my focus to college. When I was in Boy Scouts, part of their mission was to help young men experience different professions so they could make more informed decisions about their future. I was interested in the law, so earning a Law Merit Badge required me to speak with a lawyer and complete a series of exercises to better understand the profession. For a short time, I considered law as a potential career. What I found even more interesting than the law was the medical profession, specifically becoming an emergency room doctor or surgeon. Much like playing center in football, working in the ER would put me right in the middle of the action. As my senior year progressed, that became more appealing.

When my sister Shawn was in high school in North Dakota, she dated a guy who was accepted into the United States Air Force Academy. My sister also applied and she was accepted as well. The thought of attending the Air Force Academy had never crossed my mind. I knew that if I wanted to go to college, I needed to pay for it myself. My parents were not in the position to pay for anything. So, when I learned that I could receive a scholarship through the Reserve Officer Training Corps (ROTC), I jumped at the opportunity to apply. The ROTC is a program offered by all four branches of the military that provides scholarships to affiliated universities, covering the cost of tuition and books in exchange for a commitment to serve in the military after graduation.

After submitting my application in early fall 1994, I interviewed with Major Hill, the local Air Force ROTC officer. When he came to our school with his assistant, I was pulled out of class, and we met in one of the administration offices. He asked me some basic questions and confirmed the details of the application. Feeling ambitious, I told him that the three schools I was considering were Harvard, Stanford, and the University of Utah.

I was a good student with high grades. When I took the ACT during my sophomore year, I scored 32 out of 36. That put me in the 97th percentile, so I figured I didn't need to retake it because I didn't see myself scoring any higher. I also had some impressive references from my teachers. I had planned to enter the nursing program since nursing positions were more difficult to fill.

It never occurred to me that I wouldn't get the scholarship. I didn't have a backup plan. Once again, failure was not an option. Maybe it's a superpower or a character flaw, but I've always approached what I want to do with the attitude that it would work out. It hasn't always been the case, but this time it was.

In October of my senior year, I was accepted to the Air Force ROTC program at the University of Utah. I was able to earn an additional scholarship that would cover the cost of the dorm for a year, but that didn't cover the cost of food. I would be responsible for that, as well as any additional living expenses.

My friend Rick Hanna had also been accepted to the University of Utah, so we made plans to room together our freshman year. The Hannas were new to the Catholic community, originally hailing from Illinois. I had met Rich through Vince, and had spent a fair amount of time at his house during my senior year. Now, since Rich and I were attending the same college, it made sense for us to room together.

One October morning, I was driving to school on a big six-lane highway. At a light, I tried to make a left-hand turn, but there was too much traffic. I had to wait for the yellow light to turn red before there was room to get across the highway, but I had waited too long. Another car driving in the opposite direction sped forward (the driver was too distracted drinking his coffee to see me) and smacked into the front of my car before I could cross the intersection.

If I had had collision insurance, the car would have been totaled because the cost of repairs would have exceeded the Blue Book value. But I only had liability insurance, and since I was turning left and was deemed the one at fault, my insurance paid for the other car's repairs. My totaled car was towed back to our house. I couldn't afford to buy another car, and I couldn't afford to repair this one yet ($7.57 an hour doesn't go as far as one would like), so it would sit behind the garage until I had saved up enough money to fix it myself. In the meantime, I broke out my dad's old ten-speed bike.

Winter in Utah is not ideal biking weather, but I wasn't about to change my schedule or quit school just because I no longer had a car. If that meant riding my bike through the snow, so be it. Riding a bike home after work at midnight in the snow and pedaling my way through snowstorms was not enjoyable. Sometimes it got hairy, especially when riding through farm country, where there aren't many streetlights.

Once every couple of weeks, the school's athletic trainer, Mr. Stoney, would see me riding my bike to school and stop to pick me up. He lived in my neighborhood and he knew that I had wrecked my car, so he always pulled over when he saw me. He'd put my bike in the back of his vintage Dodge Ram Charger and would drive me the rest of the way to school. As a teacher, he probably wasn't supposed to do that, but he was willing to bend the rules to help a student.

Mr. Stoney was a legitimate rodeo cowboy on the senior pro circuit, so he'd often tell me about his fascinating career on the ride to school. After being nearly stomped to death, he pioneered the rodeo trend of wearing ballistic vests and helmets before making the transition to teaching.

With my schedule packed during the week, the only real time I had to work on my car was on the weekend. After six months, I had saved enough money to buy parts. Ria helped me track down what I needed at a junkyard in Provo, driving me all the way down there and back in the pickup to haul the parts I needed back to the house. That was a big help and significantly reduced the cost. The one part of the repair I couldn't do myself was straighten out the frame. I had to find an auto body shop to do that, and I was able to get it done for under $500. That was the biggest expense. The frame wasn't perfect, but they got it fairly straight. The rest, I was determined to fix myself. I had no idea what I was doing, so I had to learn on the go. The most difficult part was the electrical component and rewiring the car.

Altogether, it took about seven months to get the car up and running again, and I completed the entire project for under $1,000. My silver Accord was an interesting sight to behold, with its metallic powder-blue fender and random parts painted with black primer. It was good to have a car again, and it allowed me to put the ten-speed back in the garage, but it wasn't the last time that I'd need the bike.

The tension between my dad and Ria continued to escalate. Although I never witnessed it personally, I suspected there was more drug and alcohol use, which led to more fighting—that I did see. I didn't learn until much later the extent of the drug problems, but the fighting grew intense. One night, I was standing in between them as they started arguing. Before I realized what was happening, I was shoved out of the way. I was watching their relationship deteriorate before my eyes.

They went out together more and often stayed out late. Whenever I went out with my friends, I knew that if I made it home by one o'clock in the morning, I'd beat them home (they were always out until the bars closed at two). And then one night, my dad didn't come home at all.

After I graduated from high school in 1995, my father went on a runner—that's what we call a drinking- and drug-fueled bender. It happened every so often, and this one resulted in his disappearance for over a week. That left Ria holding the bag with a bunch of kids. Since she wasn't working, she had no way to pay for anything.

With the school year over, I started working more days at Fred Meyer. Sometimes, I'd work long ten- or twelve-hour shifts, leaving the nights free to hang out with my friends before everyone left for college. One of those days, I returned home from work in the afternoon to find the doors locked—they were never locked, not even when nobody was home. On the front porch, I saw a stack of household bills with a note from Ria, saying that I had to pay these bills or my belongings would be left on the porch.

What? Where did this come from? I was shocked. Never before had I been asked to pay the bills. Who asks their eighteen-year-old son to pay their bills? That's crazy! And what did she expect me to do with the bills on the porch? Nothing about this made any sense.

I hadn't been spending much time at the house and I had missed a lot of family meals, so I wasn't sure exactly what was going on between my dad and Ria. It didn't surprise me to learn they had money problems—drugs, alcohol, and partying are not cheap pastimes. Still, this note didn't make any sense. I thought I was on good terms with Ria. Why would she do this?

The car was gone and nobody was home, so I couldn't speak with her. I had no way to get in contact until she returned home that night, so I went over to a friend's house. I weighed my options and considered helping. I still had my job at Fred Meyer; I had some money saved in the bank, but that was for college. When I called the bank, I was frustrated to learn that Ria had also called, asking how much money was in my account. Her name was on the account because I had opened it when I was a minor. I was now eighteen. It turned out that the amount she was asking for was equivalent to what I had in my bank account. I would have nothing left if I paid these bills.

Later that night, I returned home to find the door unlocked and Ria in the living room with the kids. She asked if I would pay the bills. I told her, "No." I went to my room and that was it. She didn't say anything else and I didn't ask, but I knew this wasn't over. Ria was never one to make idle threats. I went to bed, got up early, and went to work the next day. Sure enough, when I returned home after my shift, all my stuff was sitting in black plastic trash bags on the side of the road. I felt numb, but also a small part of me felt relieved. I was finally free from this madhouse.

That was a turning point. I no longer had a place to live for the rest of the summer and the structured life and responsibilities that had helped me to thrive had ended. I would be on my own from here on out. Luckily, my car was fixed. I packed up my belongings and left to find a new place to live until college started in the fall. I also made sure to change banks!

CHAPTER 4

Wandering without a Guide

AS A young man growing into an adult, it's natural to look toward another man or group of men to help bring you along. That is true in cultures all over the world; older men bring the young boys along. I believe men demonstrate love by teaching skills and passing on their knowledge. Sometimes, that love is healthy, and other times, it's not, but in our society today, we've disrupted that process. Part of it has to do with the disintegration of the traditional family. Divorce and children being born out of wedlock is more common today than it was in previous generations, which means many young men don't have positive role models in the home.

Many of the men and male role models during my childhood disappeared. The positive ones, like Father Bitzer and Father Rizzo, were only in my life for a short period before moving on. Others either abandoned ship or, like my father, were unavailable. Some were just plain unstable. Ron, the man my mom married, was known for pulling a .44 Magnum on people who drove too fast down his road. He once held a knife to my throat. He smoked pot around us kids and walked around the house in his jockstrap. That wasn't a man whom I could look up to.

As a result, I was more comfortable talking to women, and I've had many women become that positive role model and provide guidance for me over the years.

Jeanette LaFors was my US history teacher when I lived in California. She had a greater influence on my writing than anyone else because she insisted that our class essays not be boring. Therefore, we had to use active language. We were allowed only three passive sentences per essay before she deducted points. That taught me how to write in an active voice, and it has served me well.

Karen Minor was my AP European history teacher and Model UN adviser when I lived in Utah. She was animated and bombastic—definitely not a boring history teacher. I always felt like I could talk to her, and she was willing to be real. During my senior year, I had taken a girl to a dance and I had thought it went well, but Karen Minor was able to share some interesting feedback that made me realize the dance hadn't gone as well as I had thought. It turns out the other girl thought I was "all hands." I don't recall being handsy, but I appreciated that Mrs. Minor was willing to tell me the truth.

After I was kicked out of the house and forced to fend for myself, the most influential and supportive person in my life was Deborah Marcus, the mother of my close friend Vince.

Vince's father was an executive and Deborah was a stay-at-home mom. She was tall, with dark, shoulder-length hair and an oval face that never saw much makeup. The Marcuses were an upper-class family who had a much different perspective on life, one that was foreign to me. The way I was raised, if you wanted something, you had to earn it and get it for yourself. If the Marcuses' kids wanted something, their parents would help them figure out how to get it. That was true for everything from a car to college. The Marcuses clearly cared about the long-term well-being of their children and wanted them to be successful. In contrast, I was raised by parents who viewed their role as providing for their children's basic needs—food, clothing, and shelter—until they reached the age of eighteen, after which those children were no longer their responsibility. That was how they had been raised. They didn't have support from their parents and so they grew up believing they could only rely on themselves. And that was how they raised us.

Deborah Marcus understood that I was raised in a different environment, which is why she always looked out for me and invited me over for dinner. At times, she felt like a second mom, so when I asked if I could stay with them after I was kicked out, she agreed. It sounded like a good idea at first, but I was only there a few days before Vince left for boot camp. Then, I was alone with his parents in his house. I was only there at night, since I was out working most of the day. Still, I'm sure it was an inconvenience.

I had been grinding it out at Fred Meyer through the entire school year, putting in lots of hours and working late-night shifts. At the start of the summer, a department head position became available and I informed management that I was interested in the role. It came with a pretty hefty raise—from $7.50 an hour to $12 an hour—but they didn't offer me the job. When I asked about it, I was told they found someone who was a better fit. In fairness, they were probably right. Still, it left me in a difficult position.

When I was younger, I always told my dad that I never wanted to do what he did for a living. I was never going to be an ironworker or work construction. However, living in the Marcuses' guest room and trying to save money for college, I realized that I could earn twice as much by working in construction. So, I went down to the union hall and asked what I needed to do to start.

Construction was my dad's world. My father was overseeing work at the convention center as a foreman. He didn't get me the job, but they all knew who I was over there. It was a big enough jobsite that I wouldn't be working directly for him. Besides, this wasn't a career path; it was just a job to get me through the summer. But there was one catch: I needed a permission slip signed by both my parents before I could be hired.

"I'm eighteen," I said. "Why do I need my parents' permission?"

I was told something about it being a dangerous job. It didn't make sense, but if I wanted to work, I needed to fill out the form.

I made an awkward call to my dad and Ria and arranged to meet them at the Fred Meyer parking lot. They arrived, used the back of my car to sign the form, and left. No one said a word about what had happened or the current situation.

As with many trade jobs, I began with hands-on training. That involved doing the easy tasks so you can learn before taking on more complicated responsibilities that eventually require additional training and qualifications. So, for that summer, I was the grunt. I worked mainly in the giant ballrooms, specifically putting together and adjusting the level of the support structures and steel beams that comprised the ceiling grid. It took a lot of effort to ensure everything was level.

Then, for a while, I was assigned to the fireproofing repair crew. That involved flinging and troweling fire-retardant material onto the steel where the fire retardant had been damaged. In the case of a fire, the flames won't have direct contact with the steel, which can cause it to buckle. The job required going over the steel multiple times to ensure it was completely covered—essentially, it was the job nobody else wanted to do.

Yet there was a true sense of community and camaraderie among the crew. They all liked my dad and welcomed me into the fold. If I pulled my weight and did my best, the veterans treated me well. And there was no shortage of colorful characters. Wildcat Bill was only in his late forties but had the soul of a dirty old man. He had been around the block and told me stories about his escapades working in Nevada and everything that went on "back in the day."

I have no idea if my dad went home to live with Ria that summer, but I did see him at work. We never discussed what had happened at home, but he knew where I was living. About two weeks into my stay at the Marcus house, Deborah helped me navigate an encounter with him that became one of my most painful memories of that period.

It was in the afternoon, and I was alone, playing video games in Vince's room. Deborah had been outside but walked in to track me down. From the look on her face, I could immediately tell that something was wrong. "Your dad's outside," she told me. "He's high, he's going to ask you for money, and I need you to tell him 'No.'"

I reluctantly went outside, and sure enough, there was my dad, disheveled and strung out. He looked terrible—it was the worst I had ever seen him. I was sad, upset, and confused by the whole situation. I didn't know what to feel as I watched him struggle to stay on his feet. As expected, he asked for money and I told him no. He grew angry, said a bunch of nasty things to me, and then stormed off. It was all over very quickly.

Saying no is one of the hardest things I've had to do. Had Deborah not told me to do that beforehand, I probably would have given him money. I wasn't sure if I had made the right decision or not and I was too upset to consider what I should or could have done differently.

The situation proved too much for Deborah Marcus. I could tell that she was uncomfortable with what had happened. This was not her world. Not long after, she sat me down and told me that it would be best if I moved on. She didn't give me an explanation, and I didn't need one. I understood and was grateful to her for letting me stay. That's when I called my soon-to-be roommate, Rich Hanna, about staying with him until we both went off to college.

The University of Utah was located on a sprawling campus set on the side of a sloping mountainside in Salt Lake City. From the first day, I was overwhelmed. Not by the course load, but by the unstructured freedom, specifically all the free time I suddenly had on my hands. When I was in high school, every hour of every day was accounted for. I was up early, off to school, headed to football practice, and then finished the day with a shift at work. I was on the move until midnight every weekday and out of the house most weekends. The little free time I had was spent doing schoolwork.

In college, classes were held a few times a week. I wasn't playing sports, I wasn't working a job, and the ROTC commitment was only once a week, so I was never that busy. I was out of my comfort zone and didn't know what to do with myself.

My grades soon began to suffer, primarily due to the classes I was enrolled in. I had received college credit for the AP courses I took in high school, so I wasn't taking normal entry-level college courses. Instead, I was taking challenging courses like organic chemistry and calculus. These extremely difficult classes exposed all the gaps in my education, the direct result of bouncing between different schools with different curricula. I struggled, and I didn't perform well. It didn't help that I was drinking and partying more than ever.

Getting kicked out had also cast a cloud over my first semester. I felt alone. Rich and I were roommates on campus, but he did his thing, and I did mine. Many of my fellow students went home on the weekends, but I didn't have a home to return to. I wasn't going to church every Sunday like I used to. Sometimes I slept in too late. Other times I felt too ashamed to go; I made it two or three times a month.

I was only nineteen, but I had no direction. I had lost my way and drifted from my purpose to know, love, and serve God. I knew that something had to change, so in February of my freshman year, I withdrew from college. I needed to reconnect with my faith and think about my future, and the best place to do that was back in California.

Whenever we stayed with Grandpa Des and Grandma Mitze in San Carlos, we would attend church at Saint Aloysius in nearby Campbell. Some of the priests at Saint Aloysius would later travel to Utah to perform Latin Mass in our community. That church had since moved to the mountains up in Los Gatos, about fifteen miles outside San Jose. (My father had gone up there to help them convert the barn into a church.) In addition to the church, they also had a retreat center. I was familiar with the community and knew a few of the people staying at the retreat center, so I asked if they would take me in and help me get squared away. They agreed. I left the Honda with my parents and boarded a flight to San Jose.

Saint Aloysius hosted retreats a few times a month. In addition to their main church, they had a residence for the priests and a large kitchen that served the community. About ten people lived there to help maintain the grounds. The church received funding from donations, so nobody was paid. Once I moved in, I took on whatever jobs needed to be done.

It was while staying at the religious house that I met Father Brian Hawker. A tall, sturdy man in his mid-forties, Father Hawker had been raised Catholic. He had attended a Minor Seminary in Chicago, which is like a high school for boys who aspire to become priests. He then attended the Major Seminary and, after being ordained, became an assistant pastor in Chicago, where he was paid a reasonable salary. The Church provided his house and car.

Father Hawker wanted to celebrate the Latin Mass and he did so in various communities. That put him at odds with his bishop, who told him that if he wanted to keep celebrating the Latin Mass, he would need to leave the diocese. So, he left. He gave up his salary, his house, and his car and moved into the religious house in Los Gatos, where he could celebrate the Latin Mass and better assist the people.

When I first met him, I spent a considerable amount of time helping him with his Gregorian chant. It was terrible. Eventually, he opened up to me about his struggles with insomnia and depression. Father Hawker had chosen God over everything else. He had given up his income, retirement, and worldly possessions to live in this religious house and work with the SSPX. He had a strained relationship with his parents and siblings. That challenged him, and I think he still felt like an outsider. You often think that priests or other successful people have it all figured out. But Father Hawker didn't have it all figured out, and he was okay with that. He never tried to hide it. That's what made him so relatable.

Leaving college put me in a better place mentally and spiritually. By getting to know God better—loving Him and serving Him—I was closer to living the life I was supposed to live, but something was missing. I had been a Catholic for seven years, and I was still struggling with my sins. Now, I was living in a religious house and going to church every day. I had everything I could possibly need to resolve this issue, and it still wasn't going away. I wondered if that would ever change.

In June 1996, I was four months into my stay at Saint Aloysius when I got a message from someone I never expected to hear from—Ria. She phoned the house, and it was Father Hawker who answered and spoke with her. After getting off the phone, Father Hawker came to find me. He explained how my dad had gone on another runner. Ria wanted to know if I would consider coming home to help pay the bills, so they didn't lose the house.

I wasn't surprised my father had disappeared again, but after everything that had happened, I was surprised to hear from Ria. I wasn't angry at her—I was more frustrated at my father for disappearing again. What I should do: help my family or stay the course?

Conflicted, I prayed on the decision for two days. Then I spoke with Father Hawker, who was clear about his thoughts. "You're looking for a vocation, and this would impede that. But family comes first. You have to support your family. So if you can do something to help, you should."

For me, it came down to forgiveness, which is a prominent theme in Catholicism and what distinguishes it from other religions. The absolute necessity to forgive others is clearly laid out in the "Our Father" prayer Jesus gave us in the Bible. Later, Saint Peter asked Jesus how many times he should forgive his brother, and Jesus responded, "Not seven times, but seventy-seven times." That means there is no ceiling on forgiveness.

This concept is best summed up in the parable of the unforgiving servant, the story of a servant who owed his master a lifetime of wages. When it came time for him to pay, the servant didn't have the money. The servant and his family faced a lifetime of imprisonment, so he begged his master for forgiveness, and forgiveness was granted. The newly freed servant ventured out into the world and soon came across a fellow servant who happened to owe him money—a trivial amount compared to his previous debt. However, the servant failed to show his fellow servant the same grace and lashed out, demanding payment. When they were both brought before the master, it was the servant who had been forgiven that was punished.

While the issues between us may seem significant, in the grand scheme of things, they are small compared to the sins we've committed and that have been forgiven. In turn, we should forgive others. If not, we'll eventually pay the price.

I had forgiven Ria for kicking me out. True forgiveness occurs in our soul when we're specific with our intentions and release the moral "debt" someone owes us. I had made peace with what had occurred and I wanted to move forward. (Also, I'm not good at holding grudges.) I was nineteen years old and I still didn't have any plans for my life. My time at Saint Aloysius helped, but I never planned to stay there long-term. I knew that if I went back home, I could get a job working construction. And with that money, I could make a meaningful impact to help support my family. I could always return once they were back on their feet. So, with that in mind I flew back home to Utah, hoping to do something good.

I joined a construction crew that was building the new state courthouse in Salt Lake City. The car I had left with my parents had been destroyed by drug dealers thanks to my father's runner-related activities. That meant I didn't have transportation. If I was going to work in Salt Lake City, then I needed to live there.

I reached out to my friend Steve Brousard, whose sister I knew through the Latin Mass community. Steve was an interesting character. He had an art degree from the University of Texas, but worked as a union carpenter, doing drywall and metal-stud framing, so he knew my dad through construction. At the time, he was remodeling a duplex in the area. He had redone all the wiring, so the place was stripped down to the bare studs. In the backyard, Steve had decorated some trees with twelve- to eighteen-inch ears and nose sculptures from one of his art projects. It was an eccentric place, and that's where I stayed for the next few months, sleeping on a hardwood floor. Ria brought up my ten-speed bike so I could travel back and forth from work.

My father wasn't the foreman on this job; however, I had worked with many of the guys on the crew at the convention center. Some of them knew what had happened and took me under their wing, saying, "I'm sorry this had to happen to you, kid." It was a little strange, but they were on my side and they helped me along.

The job wasn't easy, and I had my fair share of mishaps. I was responsible for welding the metal decking for a dome and cutting the pie-shaped pieces to fit it. I was young and I didn't know what I was doing. It was while wielding a giant demolition saw with a high-powered motor and fourteen-inch blade that red-hot sparks flew directly onto my pant leg. After a few minutes, I looked down and saw that my pants were on fire. I put it out, but too late. I had burned the fabric up to my knees. I walked around like that for the rest of the day and caught plenty of flak for it.

The job paid $12 an hour, so I was making about $1,920 a month before taxes. I sent $800 of that back to Ria to pay the bills. That was almost half my paycheck, but I was living rent-free, so I could afford it for the time being. My dad eventually went back home a few months later, and that's when I stopped sending money. He always went back, and Ria always took him back because she had six mouths to feed. She knew that divorcing my dad and then trying to chase him down for child support wouldn't work.

After saving enough money, I rented a quirky, ground-floor studio apartment in the Sky Harbor apartment complex near the Salt Lake City airport. This was back when there wasn't much development in that area. I didn't have a bed; I slept on a hammock made of salvaged steel from the jobsite. I didn't have furniture; I had large, industrial-sized wire spools laid out and stacked to serve as makeshift shelving.

Soon it was winter. Not having a car made it difficult to do anything in Salt Lake City and it was too cold to ride my bike back and forth to work every day. I borrowed $2,000 from my mom to purchase a used Honda Accord to commute to work.

I don't know if it was the freezing cold weather, the job, or both, but I was starting to lose my way away again. I didn't want to keep working in construction. I knew I was capable of more, so I left. I also questioned whether I wanted to return to religious life. Celibacy was a nonnegotiable for the Church and, as a twenty-year-old, that wasn't very appealing. I briefly went back to the ROTC. I took night classes. I even tried my hand at selling cars. Nothing felt right.

When my lease was up, I had a choice to make. I could renew the lease and remain in Salt Lake, but I was going nowhere there. I could move back in with my dad and Ria, but our relationship was not the same, and theirs was not a healthy environment. The only friend I considered staying with was Vince Marcus, but he wasn't in a position to have a roommate. I was in desperate need of another change and a fresh start. Where could I go?

My mom's older brother, Dennis, had been a branch manager for Apollo Piping before moving to Fargo in 1994 to take a promotion. He had married a woman named Vicky, and the two lived in Belfield, North Dakota. Vicky had an independent streak; she didn't care what anybody else thought. When my sister Shawn left the Air Force Academy, she moved in with Aunt Vicky for a while to complete her college degree from the University of North Dakota in Dickinson.

I had been up to their house once before over Christmas break during my senior year. I spent my time playing cribbage and eating oyster stew with Uncle Dennis. He had since passed away, and Vicky's brother Wayne had moved into the house with her. She had always been supportive, and I knew I could talk to her about anything. I called Aunt Vicky and asked if I could stay with her and Wayne. Without hesitation, she told me that it wasn't a problem.

To my father's credit, he had straightened himself out. He had tried to rebuild his marriage and his career. I didn't see him, so I couldn't tell how well he was doing. He had attempted to reconcile with me by giving me a 1970 Honda 350 street bike as a goodwill gesture. He felt guilty about destroying my car and gave it to me as a peace offering.

In June 1997, I sold the Accord and drove that Honda 350 over 1,000 miles from Salt Lake City all the way to Fargo, North Dakota.

After I arrived in Fargo, I immediately began searching for a job. I received two offers on the same day. The first was a night shift at a steel fabrication plant; the second was at a photographic film store. I figured I could work the day shift at one job and the night shift at the other, so I accepted both offers to earn extra money. Of course, that didn't work out. I had no idea how exhausted I would be after the night shift and when I didn't show up the next day at the film store, the owner called my aunt looking for me. That was the only time Vicky got upset with me.

"What's going on here?" she asked. "Did you take two jobs?"

"Yeah," I admitted.

"You can't take two jobs and not show up for one. That's not professional."

"I know. I'm sorry."

"How much is the guy at the film store paying you anyway?"

"Like $7.25 an hour."

"Screw him. You're not working there." She was right. (I've always shared her frustration with employers who don't pay their workers a fair wage.)

So, I quit the film store and kept the night-shift job. I worked there for the next two months. The late hours didn't allow much of a social life, so I spent most of my time figuring out what to do next. I was flailing without direction. The responsibility for my actions still lay with me, so in my head, this was all my fault. I believed I was not a disciplined person; how could I fix that? What could I do to acquire the habit of self-discipline and create a more ordered life? Just getting a job wouldn't cut it, and the Air Force ROTC was only a couple of hours one day a week.

My answer was to join the Marines. I didn't tell my parents, but I did tell Vicky. She agreed that I needed to grow up, so it sounded like a good idea to her.

Why the Marines? Well, if you want the best GI Bill, you join the Air Force. If you don't know what you're doing with yourself, you join the Army. If you're from Nebraska and want to see the world, you join the Navy. But if you want to *be the best*, you join the Marines.

I wanted to be the best.

When I walked into the Marine Corps recruiting office in Fargo, I immediately took a liking to the recruiter. I don't remember his name, but he was a fun guy who made a lasting impression. He was a gunnery sergeant who reminded me of Clint Eastwood's character in *Heartbreak Ridge*. At six foot two with broad shoulders and his hair cut high and tight, he was a cross between the older brother I never had and the uncle who tells dirty jokes when your parents aren't around.

When I told him I was considering the Naval ROTC program, he dismissed it. "You don't want to do that. You want to enlist first and learn what it's *really* like to be a Marine before you put on bars." I wasn't even in the office an hour before he had convinced me. As someone in desperate need of guidance and healthy, positive role models, I enlisted on the spot.

The following week, after I passed my mandatory physical and medical tests, I went to the Military Entrance Processing Station in

Sioux Falls, South Dakota. That's where I took the Armed Services Vocational Aptitude Battery (ASVAB), a standardized test given to enlistees to determine what they're capable of.

Before shipping out for boot camp in San Diego, I met with the recruiter again to discuss where I wanted to be assigned for the next four years after boot camp. (They determine this beforehand, because once you ship out, your path is set.)

I knew that I didn't want to ride a desk or be a mechanic. I was looking for excitement and adventure. I had been reading books about the Marines and might have romanticized the experience a little bit. That's why I told him that I wanted to join the infantry.

"I don't think you heard us correctly. You can do any job you want after boot camp. What would you like to do?"

"Infantry," I insisted. I think the gunny saw my potential and thought I was squandering it by going into the infantry. Or maybe he was trying to hit a recruiting target for hard-to-fill roles. Who knows?

It was 1997. There was no ongoing military conflict at the time so I knew I wouldn't be stationed in a war zone. The last conflict, Desert Storm, had been in the early 1990s, and while the United States was involved in a military conflict in the Balkans, they weren't sending a massive number of troops over there. (This was before 9/11 and was considered peacetime.)

In my mind, joining the infantry was the best way to develop discipline and build my character. The Marines are considered the sharpest and most disciplined branch of the military. To put it another way: Air Force boot camp is six weeks. Army boot camp is eight weeks. But the Marine boot camp is twelve weeks. For the Marines, it's not good enough that you just know the basics. They use that time to get you dialed in. Every Marine is a rifleman, no matter what the job, whereas in the Air Force, 80 percent of the people are support personnel. Also, their sergeants seemed to have colorful stories, and their uniforms look better. I was there to be the best, and I wanted to milk the experience for all it was worth.

PART II

LOOKING FOR PEACE

CHAPTER 5

Five Weeks to Revelation

I ARRIVED in San Diego in August 1997 hoping the Marines would do for me what I couldn't—rebuild me from the ground up. After years of false starts and failed attempts at finding direction, I was ready to surrender control and let the Corps forge me into someone new. But as I would soon discover, you can't outsource the work of becoming whole. The Marines would break me down, but when they couldn't put me back together, I'd find myself more lost than ever. This began a spiral that would take me further from God than I'd ever been. What I didn't understand at the time was that no institution, no matter how disciplined or demanding, could do the internal work that only I could do.

It wasn't yet dawn when I got off the plane in San Diego. I was twenty years old, slightly older than the recent high school graduates who were also arriving for boot camp at one of the only Marine Corps training centers in the country.

Noncommissioned officers were waiting at the San Diego International airport to greet me and the other recruits. There were close to one thousand recruits in our rotation: ten to twelve squads of eighty to ninety recruits each. Each week, a new rotation began with a new batch of recruits. Together, we boarded a bus for the short trip to the nearby Marine Corps Recruit Depot.

On the bus, I heard some recruits second-guessing their decision and by the look on the faces of others, it was obvious they were experiencing a *What did I get myself into?* moment. I never had that moment. I viewed the next twelve weeks of boot camp as a form of self-help because I needed the discipline; I needed to be whipped into shape. Who better to do that than the Marine Corps? I went in thinking, "What skills am I currently lacking, and how do I acquire those skills?"

At the training facility, we piled off the bus to begin the intake process, which was designed to strip away any disorder and randomness and start us on the path to military order and discipline. Nothing was left up to the individual.

First, we stood in a line of yellow footprints painted on the sidewalk—they didn't even trust us to form proper lines on our own.

Then, we moved into a line for medical examinations, as each recruit was processed through a series of physical assessments with clinical efficiency.

Next was the line for the supply depot to pick up our uniforms and all the supplies we would need, each item checked off a standardized list.

The haircuts followed the same assembly-line format—five barbers, each manning a separate chair, quickly gave each recruit the same buzz cut to keep the line moving without pause.

We lined up again to be ushered into a giant warehouse where drill sergeants assigned each of us a spot on the floor to keep our personal belongings until the end of boot camp. I handed over everything but my brown scapular—a cloth necklace that I had worn since becoming a Catholic.

We recruits were all permitted one phone call, and that required getting in yet another line. Even the call was regimented: There was a time limit given to read a script that informed the person we were speaking to that we made it safely to camp. That was it. No small talk allowed. When I reached the front of that line, I called my mom.

The barracks (or squad bay as it was called) I was assigned to had fifty bunk beds—I was given a bottom bunk. That first day, we were taught how to make our bunk so that it looked like everyone else's bunk. We all had white sheets with a drab olive-green wool blanket that shed fibers everywhere. That proved to be a problem since we had to keep the squad bay immaculate.

Everyone was given their own footlocker, just like in the film *Full Metal Jacket*. Pull-up bars were set up around the bay.

Just outside the squad bay was the "head"—a long line of urinals and about eight toilets with no doors, just dividers between the toilets. Everything was out in the open.

The shower room had two large central pipes with eight showerheads emerging from each pipe. When you have ninety guys lining up to take a shower (and there was always a line), you get used to standing under the showerhead, getting wet, washing quickly, finding a spot to rinse off, and then getting out of the way for the next recruit. There would be no long, hot showers.

Everything the Marine Corps did was highly efficient. It had to be. And from that day on, our routine was the same.

We were up at 5:00 a.m. to exercise and drill before breakfast in the mess hall.

Then, a second round of exercise and drills before classes and lunch.

Followed by a third round of exercise and drills before the next set of classes and dinner.

All of our days were well structured, and that's what I had asked for, so I couldn't complain. But it was demanding and difficult. I wouldn't say I enjoyed myself, but I was being productive. Most importantly, I had a plan for the next four years. That alone put me in a better place mentally and spiritually than I was before I left.

Two weeks into camp, the drill sergeant, Sergeant Cannedy

(pronounced "Kennedy"), called me into his office. "I'm going to need you to take off that necklace, son."

He was referring to the brown scapular I wore around my neck. This was an issue. Marine recruits are not supposed to wear jewelry. We are not supposed to wear anything that makes an individual stand out from the group. The Marines want everyone to be on the same level, to wear the same thing. Everyone is equal, no exceptions.

"I can't do that, sir."

"Can you explain yourself?"

"It's not a necklace, sir."

"Then what is it?"

I told him the story behind the scapular, how the Virgin Mary appeared to Saint Simon Stock in the thirteenth century as a sign of his love for her. (That's why some brown scapulars have the phrase, "He who dies wearing this scapular shall not suffer eternal fire," written on them. I wore it as a reminder of that pledge: If I stick with God, He'll have my back.)

"Okay, son. That's all."

Once he learned that it was a religious symbol and I wasn't a kid showing off his jewelry, the matter didn't escalate further, and it never came up again. However, it didn't go unnoticed by the others.

Maybe a quarter of the recruits were Catholics, but few were devout, practicing Catholics. Some noticed that I wore an item that wasn't typically allowed, something that becomes obvious when you're showering every day with a group of guys. A few recruits approached me wanting to know more about the scapular, or even follow suit. And because I was slightly older, they sought me out for religious encouragement. After a little while, I became the person recruits came to when asking questions about the Church or for spiritual guidance.

There was a chapel on the base, and there was a Catholic Mass held every Sunday that we were allowed to attend. Throughout the week, I would meet up with the other Catholic recruits during our free time to pray the rosary. It wasn't the ideal environment to practice religious devotion, but we tried to stay the path and do what any good Catholic would do in the situation. And just because some of the younger guys looked to me for guidance, that didn't mean that I had it all figured out. I was being tested just as much as everyone else.

The purpose of boot camp is to deliberately break down civilian recruits so the Corps can rebuild them and mold them into elite Marines. It's a difficult process to endure, no matter how physically and mentally strong you are.

My breaking point occurred a few weeks in when the drill sergeant caught someone hiding food in their footlocker. We had returned to the squad bay from the mess hall that night, ready to go to bed, only to find Sergeant Cannedy waiting there to tell us that we had to dump out our footlockers and repack them. When you think you're done for the day, and all you want to do is lie on your bunk and go to sleep for the night, the last thing you want to hear is that the day isn't over.

Hearing our punishment, my stomach dropped. I felt ill. All I wanted to do was sleep. Eighty-seven out of eighty-eight people did everything right, but because one person broke a rule, we had to spend the next half hour unpacking and repacking our footlockers, over and over. It was unreasonable and, in that moment, I was on the verge of tears. Luckily, I was able to compose myself, but my emotions got the best of me and I cracked.

Every recruit experiences something like this during boot camp. It's impossible to avoid because the potential infractions are endless. Someone leaves their footlocker unlocked. Someone doesn't make their bed correctly. Someone brings cookies back from the mess hall. Someone does a drill wrong. It doesn't matter what the issue is or who screwed up; we have to stop what we're doing and deal with the punishment, be it running another two miles or dumping out and repacking our footlockers. Nobody wants to be "that guy," and that heightens everyone's sense of responsibility to the rest of the team. Still, it happens, every day, and those situations can become too much. It's why some recruits don't make it through. Those who can overcome adversity and recover from setbacks typically settle in for the long haul.

I never tried to smuggle food into the squad bay, but I did find a way to smuggle in reading material. You're not allowed to take books with you to boot camp. I wanted to read at night, so I talked my mom into ripping out twenty pages of a paperback and mailing it to me each day along with a letter. Every day, I would get the next twenty pages of the first book in Robert Jordan's *Wheel of Time* series. It wasn't a big secret. The drill sergeants knew what was happening because they went through the mail to make sure I didn't have pornography or some other form of contraband in my letters. They let it go. The book was long and reading it in twenty-page increments would take most of boot camp. But I would never finish it.

The first five weeks of camp went well, or at least as well as expected. I was in the best shape of my life and was really proud of how well I was handling the physical fitness aspect of boot camp. At the start of week six, I came down with a stomach bug.

It hit me in the evening and I spent all night on the toilet with diarrhea. They don't put you on sick call for diarrhea, so I wasn't excused from drills the next day. I had to suck it up when it came time for our two-mile morning run. Before we left the squad bay, I ran to the toilet. When I emerged, I was already behind the rest of the unit and was getting yelled at by Sergeant Sugarman. Once I caught up with the group, I had to peel off again to one of the field latrines.

I quickly learned that a stomach bug is not the ailment you want to endure before going on a two-mile run in the eighty-five-degree Southern California heat. I ended up at the back of the battalion, just in front of the battalion leadership. By the end of the run, I was delirious—light-headed with spotty vision. I dropped to the ground, pawing at whatever was in reach.

The battalion commander stood over me. "Son, what are you doing?" he screamed.

I said the first thing that came to mind. "I'm looking for my glasses, sir."

"They're on your face, son." He then turned and shouted to the group behind him, "Get him to the infirmary!"

I don't remember how we got to the emergency room at the base hospital. Clearly, the doctors knew something was wrong upon my arrival because they put me in an ice bath. My temperature had skyrocketed to 108 degrees. I was suffering from heatstroke. Over the next few hours, I was in and out of consciousness. At one point, I remembered Sergeant Sugarman pulling on my chest hair, yelling at me that I didn't have permission to die.

It's true what they say about "seeing the light." It felt like my time might be up. I was moving toward the light (or maybe it was moving toward me), but then I thought, "God, I can't go yet. I still owe my mom $2,000 for the money she loaned me to buy the car!" It's an absurd thing to worry about when on death's door, but I did feel bad about owing my mom money.

After the doctors got my temperature down, I was transferred from the ER to the base ICU. Interestingly, the Corps had phoned my dad and Ria, who didn't even realize I had enlisted in the Corps until they received that call.

I had my own room in the ICU, though I don't remember much about my time there—I was weak and bedridden, but stable. I had a catheter because I couldn't make it to the bathroom on my own.

The Corps typically doesn't make it easy to quit. Still, I suspected I would be discharged. Once you've had a heatstroke, your temperature regulation system doesn't work the same again, so you're more susceptible to future heatstrokes. When you're young, it's easy to think that you're invincible. But my experience in the ICU was a good reminder that I was not as tough as I thought.

It was while I was in the ICU that I had a chance to speak with the Protestant chaplain stationed at the recruit depot. I hadn't met him before; he was a kind middle-aged man in a clerical suit who was making the rounds to check on people in need. Suffering from heatstroke felt like a warning to stop running away from what God wanted me to do. I told the chaplain that I believed the experience was a sign from God, letting me know that I was supposed to go in a different direction.

Somehow, Father Hawker from Saint Aloysius had heard through the grapevine that I was in the ICU and got in contact with me. We spoke over the phone and agreed that I needed to regroup and get back on track. We didn't discuss returning to Saint Aloysius. I think it would have been too early. In religious life, you should be healthy before committing to God. If you're not, it can be a sign that you're not supposed to be there. Before I did anything, I needed to rebuild myself.

Before enlisting, I had been staying with my aunt in Fargo, but there were few churches. I often thought about my time spent living among the priests at Immaculate Conception in Post Falls, Idaho, when I was thirteen. It was a church with a strong sense of community and a place where I knew I could find healthy support. It felt like the best place for me to go and rebuild. That, to me, was a clear sign, or rather the direction God wanted me to go. I didn't know what I was going to do when I got there, but that's where I would go. That was the extent of my plan.

After I spent three days spent recovering in the ICU and planning my next steps, the Marine Corps kindly informed me that I wasn't fit for duty. They released me on an entry-level discharge, which meant that I was going home without any military record—it wasn't good, but it wasn't bad either. Once discharged, I spent my last few days of camp isolated from the rest of the recruits, assigned to menial labor while they processed my paperwork and arranged for me to travel home.

Heatstroke was a fluke, bad luck, or maybe even a blessing, depending on how you looked at it, but I wasn't disappointed. Had I finished boot camp and joined the infantry as planned, I would have made a decent Marine. Not the strongest or the toughest, but respectable. Who knows what my path might have been like if I had become an infantryman? Maybe this was the best-case scenario: come to boot camp, get my butt kicked for five weeks, and then be sent home.

My experience in boot camp wasn't a failure; it was an opportunity for rebirth.

I returned to my aunt's house in Fargo in October 1997, but I wasn't there for long—just a few days to regroup before traveling to Idaho. I cashed the pay I received for five weeks of boot camp ($1,000 after they deducted for expenses), sold my motorcycle, and bought a black-and-white 1976 GMC Jimmy from my aunt that used to be my Uncle Dennis's hunting rig.

On my drive to Post Falls, Idaho, I stopped in Butte, Montana, where my father was working a job and living out of a motel. He knew the ironworker union apprenticeship coordinator who worked out of Spokane and gave me his number for when I got settled and needed to work. Post Falls was thirty minutes east of Spokane, Washington—the largest city in the area.

When I arrived in Post Falls the next day, I drove straight to Immaculate Conception. I hadn't called ahead or spoken to anyone. A cell phone wasn't in my budget, and I didn't have access to the internet, so I just went. Fortune favors the bold.

It had been eight years since I had spent a week there as a child. There had been some minor remodeling, but it was the same quaint western church that I remembered. Not much had changed except for the priests. The SSPX frequently transfers priests every couple of years so that they don't become too attached to any one community.

I had met Father Leo Boyle when he traveled to Utah to serve our community. He was Irish to the core—six feet two with thick black hair—and was now the head priest at Immaculate Conception. He remembered me as well. I inquired about a place to stay, and Father Boyle put me in touch with Rick Wheeler and Jerry Wade, two church members who were renting a room in their house.

I went to the house to meet Rick and Jerry, only to discover that it wasn't a bedroom they were renting—but a utility closet. They lived in a finished basement that Rick rented from the owners who lived in the main house above them. The basement had two bedrooms, a kitchen, and an eight-by-ten utility closet with a water heater that barely fit a twin bed. It was mine if I wanted it for $300 a month, and I wanted it. I didn't find out until later that Rick rented the entire space for $600 a month and charged both Jerry and me $300 each, so he was living rent-free while we paid the bills.

Rick and Jerry were both thirty, ten years older than I was, and were complete opposites. Rick was a classically trained vocalist who enjoyed music and fine food. Jerry was an oddball, a class clown type whom everyone loved. He was the life of the party, so it was always fun to tag along with him at various social events in town. He was a good guy to know when trying to meet people.

Living in Idaho was different. The mountains weren't nearly as high as those in Utah. Everything felt smaller and spread out. The next town was twenty miles away, so if you needed to pick up anything that wasn't a basic necessity, you'd have to drive twenty miles. When I stayed with my grandparents in California, I didn't have to travel more than thirty miles to find an ironworking job. In Idaho, that radius was 150 miles. It made work much more difficult to come by.

I was reluctant to get back into ironwork, and part of me was humiliated because I was so adamant growing up that I was never going to be an ironworker, but that was the best opportunity to make money. I reached out to Andy Phillipson, the apprenticeship coordinator whose number my father had given me. I had joined the ironworkers' union in Utah on a temporary basis and started apprenticeship school. Now that I was living in Idaho, I had to transfer my union membership to Local 14 and join the apprenticeship program under Andy. That involved 172 hours of classroom training per year for four years, and a minimum of 6,000 hours of on-the-job training before I could graduate and become a journeyman. Given the on-again-off-again nature of construction work, 1,500 hours is considered a typical year (compared to 2,000 for a normal full-time employee), so 6,000 hours translates to roughly four years of work experience before graduating from the apprentice program.

I scheduled a meeting with Andy at the training facility in Spokane, Washington. It was only a twenty-mile trip, but the Jimmy broke down on the highway and I was forced to hitchhike the rest of the way. When I finally arrived, Andy was furious.

"You can't be late in construction. That's not acceptable," he said.

"My rig broke down on the way here. It's sitting on the side of the road, about two exits from here."

"Well, then, let's go fix your rig."

He grabbed his coat and motioned me to follow him out the door. I hopped into his truck, and together we drove to where the Jimmy was parked on the highway. He poked around under the hood then drove me over to a NAPA to pick up the oil lift pump I needed. He even drove me back to my truck and helped me install it. He didn't have to do any of that, but he did. That's the kind of guy Andy was, and he soon became a really good friend.

Andy was about forty, a few years younger than my dad at the time. Being the apprentice coordinator was a thankless job; you have a limited budget while trying to train kids to do a job according to the state requirements. And the kids don't appreciate having to take time off work to get training, so they don't always come prepared or do things the proper way. Andy extended goodwill if you showed goodwill. He wanted everyone to get along and work together to improve things. If you didn't respond to his goodwill or abused his trust, he didn't have time for you. Some people didn't like him because he treated everyone equally and always did things by the book, which was frustrating at times, but he was always fair.

Through Andy, I was able to land some minor jobs here and

there. I'd get a couple of days working on rebar (the heavy, steel reinforced bars used to support concrete) for one company and then wouldn't hear anything for a few weeks until landing a couple more days working on rebar for another company.

Finding local work was difficult. I managed to get a job down in the Tri-Cities of Washington, 140 miles away. I didn't want to waste money staying in a hotel the night before, so I set out early in the morning for the drive there. The first hour of the two-and-a-half-hour drive went well. It was dark, and there were very few cars on the road. Suddenly, I looked in the rearview mirror and saw sparks flying out from underneath the Jimmy. I pulled over, wedged my way underneath the truck, and saw that the front driveline had dropped—its rear U-joint had failed. That was not something I could fix by myself on the side of the road. I needed to get to the jobsite, so I stuck out my thumb to hitch a ride.

It was four o'clock in the morning when a semitruck driver saw me broken down on the side of the road and pulled over. He drove me another hour down the highway and dropped me off at Denny's in Pasco. I walked inside and asked the waitress if there was a pay phone. She looked at me like I had just crawled out of the gutter before pointing to the back. I got on the phone and called my dad, who was working in the Tri-Cities at the time. He couldn't get me to the jobsite, but he could get me a Greyhound bus ticket to the town where my truck had broken down. That's what I decided to do.

Before leaving Denny's, I walked into the bathroom. When I saw myself in the mirror, I suddenly understood the crazy look from the waitress. Grease covered half my face, and my hair and beard had burnt patches from being under the truck. I looked awful.

I never made it to the job that day. I took the Greyhound bus back to the tiny town where my truck had broken down. I had it towed to a local garage and ended up having to stay two nights at a hotel that I couldn't afford while they shipped my driveline back to be rebuilt and rebalanced before it could be reinstalled. My attempt to earn a couple hundred dollars by driving 140 miles to that jobsite cost me a couple of thousand dollars thanks to the breakdown. Like most Americans, I didn't have cash lying around for emergencies. I had to put the repairs and the hotel on a credit card, which took me many months to pay off.

It was one problem after another with the Jimmy. Once I got the driveline fixed, the transmission went out. That meant that I couldn't work, so I started collecting unemployment until I had saved enough money to fix the transmission. I then hired a local mechanic to come by the house. It was a late winter day, and it was pouring rain. There were two inches of standing water in the driveway, yet we managed to get the Jimmy up on a tiny jack. There was barely enough room for the two of us to lay down underneath the truck and replace the transmission.

Meanwhile, my dad was now living in Utah with Ria but working in the Idaho area on a job as a precast erection foreman. When he learned that I had a place to stay in Post Falls, he asked if he could move in with me. He had since cleaned up, and while he wasn't perfect, he was at least trying to live on the straight-and-narrow path. There wasn't much room in the utility closet, and our relationship had been strained ever since I had been kicked out of the house two years prior, but I believed that helping my father was part of my duty as his son, so I agreed.

When he arrived in December 1997, we put a bedroll next to the twin bed, and that pretty much took up all the free floor space. There was no room to walk around, but we didn't spend much time there together. He worked his job, and when I had a job, I worked mine. We shared some meals, but we didn't talk much.

Even when I had reliable transportation again, there were long stretches with nothing to do, so I needed ways to occupy myself. I sang in the church Schola, which was the men's choir at Immaculate Conception. I had sung in the choir when we lived in California, and I enjoyed it, so I gave that a shot. There were ten of us and we practiced on Saturday for about two hours and then again before Mass on Sunday, so it wasn't a major commitment.

When I was at home, I watched TV, read books, and played video games on Rick's computer. Other than Jerry and Rick, I didn't make many new friends in Post Falls. I was not hyperproductive when in between jobs. And I was broke, so I basically stayed at home and ate. The local grocery store sold specialty packs of pre-seasoned rice and beans. I could then buy some chicken or meat and make myself a substantial meal for under five bucks. It seemed like a step up from ramen, which had been a dietary staple a few years earlier. Things were not going according to plan, and right on cue, I managed to completely derail my life.

I met Gloria at church. She had grown up in the Phoenix area where she had met Father Boyle and had moved to Post Falls to start anew after an unhealthy relationship. She was a vibrant Latina woman with black shoulder-length hair, tanned skin, and an hourglass figure. She was also a lot of fun to be around. That sucked me in, and I immediately fell head over heels in love, though looking back now, it was clearly lust. Our relationship escalated quickly. We were a couple of wounded young kids in their early twenties trying to live life according to the Church and failing miserably. We knew having sex was wrong, but we couldn't help ourselves, and that led to internal conflict for both of us. I was so wrapped up in this relationship that I bought a ring and proposed, and she said yes.

We had only been dating for four months, but I was regressing. I wasn't living the life I meant to live—a life aligned with and in the service of God—after leaving boot camp. Even my father saw problems with the highly sexual nature of our relationship—it was obvious. It was during one of our only honest and real talks since he had moved in that my dad convinced me that I needed to end the relationship and get away.

I broke up with Gloria (though she kept the ring) and bought a maroon Volvo 240 from a member of the church. By April 1998, I needed to move somewhere familiar where I would be able to find steady work—Grandpa Des and Grandma Mitze's house in San Carlos, California.

My dad used to work for a company called Stott Erectors. When they dissolved, Tony Stott, one of the brothers who owned the company, founded his own company, Western Construction Specialties. A few months after I settled in San Carlos, Western Construction hired my dad to lead one of the crews working on a project to erect the structural steel for an office building complex at the Sun Microsystems campus in Newark, California. That was less than thirty minutes from my grandparents' house, so my father left Idaho and moved in with us in San Carlos. He even got me a job working on that project.

Despite my reluctance to become an ironworker, there was more work available in the Northern California area, so I was begrudgingly advancing in my career. When I took this job, I had graduated to connector, which is a prestigious position in the trade. Connectors are the guys who climb up the iron to put the pieces of steel together. It was steady work that came with a hefty pay raise.

That job ended in the fall of 1998. I was offered another job working as a connector in Denver. It was a chance to earn more money than ever before and it convinced me that people believed I was good enough to do the job. I was flattered. Denver would be a new city, but the pattern was becoming familiar. Another attempt to get back on track. Another need for a fresh start.

They say that a tree falls the way it leans. I had spent my childhood moving from home to home, being shepherded between my parents. I hated it. I had wanted to stay in the same place and go to the same school. As an adult, now that I was on my own, I repeated that same pattern. I was never in one place for long. I always had the best intentions of getting my life back on track, but I still managed to get sidetracked and lose my way. I wasn't progressing, and the way I was living was unhealthy. It wasn't a matter of circumstances or bad luck. I had brought it all on myself because I was not doing what I was supposed to be doing.

I was running away from God.

Saint Thomas Aquinas once said that man is always chasing a good but sometimes chooses an inferior good over a superior good. For example, honor is good but not as good as true charity and divine love. If you choose honor over divine love, you're choosing the inferior good. That can be a form of delusion. This concept gets at the heart of human nature. Most people aren't evil for the sake of being evil. Most are chasing a good. The problem is when they get caught up chasing an inferior good without even realizing it.

I was chasing a good, but it was an inferior good. My background, early trauma, and hyper-sexualization had skewed my judgment and made it difficult to tell the difference between the two, but the picture was growing clearer. It had started in the ICU at boot camp. That's when I realized I had been seeking discipline, acceptance, and love in a place where I could find it, but by doing so, I was running away from where I should be. When I got caught up in my relationship with Gloria, I was doing the same thing.

Every step of the way, I was running away from God. Luckily, God did not turn His back on me.

My life could have turned out much worse. Many people who grew up like I did, including family members, struggled with drugs and alcohol. That can have nasty consequences. I didn't go that route. Early sexual relationships can lead to children you didn't plan for, and that complicates life very quickly. I had relationships that could have gone that way but didn't. Given those circumstances and the mistakes I made along the way, I believe that God had protected me from my stupidity.

Looking back, I am grateful for my mistakes because they were the best path to get where I am today. It's a demonstration of God's power that He can bring good out of a bad situation. Many philosophies arrive at this point, but I tend to view circumstances (both positive and negative) as happening *for* me, not *to* me. That has helped me remain positive, maintain agency, and find joy in life. I still make mistakes. It's a humbling reminder that life can be unexpected and that I am not fully in control.

The highest and best good I could pursue was to follow God or love itself. Any attempt to pursue honor, money, sex, or pleasure in place of that love was the lesser good, and it took me further away from what God wanted me to do, which was to love and serve Him.

My next step needed to be completely in line with that greater good.

CHAPTER 6

Dreaming in French

WHEN I was growing up in Utah, I would see missionaries venture out into the world to do good work in the name of God. I felt like it was my time to leave home to do good work. Moving into the religious house was always an intermediate step. I went there to reconnect with my purpose and figure out what to do next. It was never meant to be permanent. It was while working in San Carlos that I realized what I needed was something permanent.

Most Catholics are called to live a relatively normal human life—career, spouse, kids, grandkids. They marvel at the goodness of God. Others are called to follow the "Evangelical Counsels," also known as vows of chastity, poverty, and obedience. This comes from the Gospels, where Christ asks individuals to give up everything and follow Him. This bifurcated pathway is explained at length in the letters of Saint Paul, summed up by the verse, "he who gives his daughter in marriage does well, he who allows his daughter to consecrate her life to God and stay a virgin does better." I wanted to follow the Evangelical Counsels, and I wanted to do it in the best way possible.

When I was living at the religious house back in 1996, I learned about a Dominican monastery called Couvent de la

Haye-aux-Bonshommes in Avrillé, France. The more I learned, the more appealing it seemed as an option. Going there would allow me to follow the Evangelical Counsels; they didn't compromise, or believe that modern man was weak and incapable of living like a real monk. I also liked how they balanced the Active Life (serve people out in the world) with the Contemplative Life (dedicate themselves to the contemplation of God). It seemed like a good fit, but it was not a decision I could afford to take lightly.

Moving into a monastery in France *would* be the permanent step I was seeking. I was twenty-two years old and planned to devote the rest of my life to this pursuit. That meant giving up the chance to marry, to have a wife and children. It meant giving up sex and the pleasures I had been pursuing. It was a sacrifice, and one I believed to be a noble good. I made up my mind and was at peace with my decision.

In the summer of 1998, I wrote a letter of inquiry to the head of the monastery, expressing my intentions. Father Hawker sent a recommendation on my behalf. Oddly enough, I didn't have a conversation with anyone at the monastery. They requested copies of my sacramental records and checked my references, so they did their due diligence. They saw me as someone who was serious, someone who came highly recommended and who had lived in a retreat house, who had taken steps to separate himself from the world. Three months later, I was accepted. They asked when I was coming, and I made plans to arrive in January 1999. The whole process was surprisingly easy.

When you join a religious order, they agree to take you on as their responsibility. I first had to apply for a long-stay visa that allowed me to stay in France for more than ninety days. It didn't authorize me to work, and I would have to renew the visa every year that I remained in France. I picked my visa up at the French Consulate right before my trip, cutting it very close. (It wasn't ready until three days before I was scheduled to leave. That was nerve-racking.)

Father Hawker was amused that the date of my radical move, January 25, coincided with the Feast of the Conversion of Saint Paul, which marked his dramatic transformation from persecuting Catholics to becoming a devout apostle. I was excited and nervous, but more excited because I was finally doing what I was supposed to be doing. I had stopped running and sought permanence. That filled me with contentment.

My dad and Ria supported my decision. My mom had a different perspective. I wouldn't learn until later how upset she had been. She had thought I was running away to join a cult. I understand how, if you're not Catholic, and especially if you're unfamiliar with traditional Catholicism, you can get that impression. But that didn't deter me or make me question my decision.

I didn't speak French and I had never left the country. My father said he took me to Mexico and Canada, but I have no memory of it. Father Hawker spoke a little French, so when it was time for me to leave, he traveled with me to France to ensure I arrived safely.

After a long and cramped flight, we landed in Paris to meet our driver for the three-and-a-half-hour trip through the countryside to the monastery, which was in the village of Avrillé. It was a small community on the edge of farmland. I had seen a few pictures of the monastery in the brochure, but nothing prepared me for what I experienced when we arrived.

Our car crunched slowly along the gravel pathway that wound between well-maintained lawns and ancient trees. Through the windshield, I caught my first glimpse of the monastery. The ancient yellow limestone structure seemed to emerge from the rolling green countryside. Dark slate roofs covered the buildings, and the stone had weathered to a warm, cream-colored hue.

The driver brought the car to a gentle stop near the main entrance. Father Hawker and I stepped out onto the gravel. The silence was profound.

Three brothers approached us from the main building, moving with unhurried grace. They wore the traditional white robes of their order, the long habits flowing as they walked, with black cappas draped over their heads. Each bore the distinctive tonsure—a circular patch of hair shaved from the crown of his head—that marked them as friars.

The eldest brother stepped forward and greeted Father Hawker. One of the younger brothers smiled warmly at me and gestured with a sweep of his hand for us to follow him.

The heart of the monastery was its interior cloister—a square courtyard surrounded by covered walkways. The center featured a formal rose garden with planting beds arranged around a stone cross. Behind the main complex was a vegetable garden with neat rows of plants lining a dirt path that led into the forest.

The brothers led us through the heavy wooden doors and into the church, which had been built in the 1000s. As soon as I stepped inside, I felt the warmth of the candlelight. It was a Romanesque barrel-vaulted church, narrow, long, and tall—fifty feet wide and three hundred feet long with forty-foot ceilings. The only windows were three twenty-five-foot-tall lancet windows, which provided a tremendous amount of natural sunlight behind the altar. I felt pulled toward it.

Above the altar, a partially restored bright fresco made me gape with wonder. They had completed restoring part of a beautiful image of the baby Jesus sitting on Mary's lap. The Child held a scepter held in one hand and a globe in the other. It was more colorful than I would ever expect to see in an old stone church. The pews were frail benches with wooden slabs carelessly tacked to the back, so different from the elaborate, sculpted pews found in modern American churches.

After I had seen the grounds and the church, the brothers showed me to my room. There were two dormitory wings, both built in the 1600s, and another wing under reconstruction. It had been torn down during the French Revolution and the stone used to build new farmhouses for supporters of the Revolution. I would live in a building that was almost two hundred years older than my country. My room was eight by ten feet with a large window that faced the houses on the other side of the monastery wall.

There was a cot with a small mattress, a wardrobe for clothes, and a tiny desk with a wooden chair. The only other piece of furniture was a kneeler on which to pray. And these traditional French kneelers were horribly uncomfortable. The woven reed platform was just high enough so that your feet couldn't touch the floor. The front rung dug mercilessly into your shins. I learned quickly that I was better off kneeling on the floor.

There were about thirty people living in the dormitory—ten brothers who had said their vows, five student brothers (some of them novices) studying to be priests, ten lay brothers (also some of them novices) who helped with the day-to-day operations, and five fellow postulants, like me, who were studying to become novices.

As postulants, we were to wear a black cape over our regular clothes—usually slacks, a buttoned-up shirt, and a tie. I would wear that until I was allowed to take the habit and became a novice. As a novice, you're accepted as a brother and considered a friar but have yet to take your permanent vows to become a priest.

Most of the priests and novices were French, but there were brothers from all over the world. One of the postulants was Australian, and there were even a few Americans. There were always students and brothers from other religious orders who would pass through the monastery for brief stays as part of their training. Occasionally, a bishop would stay on the grounds. Dominicans are friars, not monks, which means that while they live in a monastic setting, they also venture into the community to preach and spread the faith. (Monks take a vow of stability, which confines them to the monastery until they are sent elsewhere.) The friars at our monastery were active in the community.

Everyone lived in the dormitory and ate together, but the postulants and novices were kept separate from the priests until they took their vows and it was clear they were heading in the right direction. The brothers attempted to isolate the postulants and novices from outside influences, including the other brothers. The funny thing about being Catholic is that while the Church encourages you to work toward perfection, it also recognizes and accepts the frailty of the human condition and tries to mitigate bad influences. Sometimes brothers and priests lose their fervor, get stuck in routine, or disagree with their superiors. Those attitudes could derail the formation of the new novices.

It could take anywhere from six months to a year to transition from a postulant to a novice and then another year before taking temporary vows. Then another ten years before taking the final set of vows to become a priest. Or it might not happen at all. The main criteria to become a priest were time and maturity, and those decisions were made by the brothers, specifically Father Innocent-Marie.

Father Innocent-Marie was the Father Superior in charge of the monastery. At fifty, his hair (minus the tonsure) was gray, and he had a dark complexion. He was stocky, not the stereotypical emaciated monk. He also believed that eating garlic and shallots was essential for preserving health, so he consumed several raw onions and raw cloves of garlic with every meal. As a result, he always smelled like garlic.

Under Father Innocent-Marie were a prior and a subprior. Most Dominican monasteries had a separate novice master who educated and mentored the postulants, but Father Innocent-Marie chose to take on this role himself. He believed it was crucial to educate and influence all the young men entering the community. It's not that he didn't trust the other brothers to do a good job, but it was a small community, and they were spread thin, so he wanted everyone to focus on their responsibilities.

Today, it's easy to equate love with sex, but in a healthy society, you can experience real love without sex. Father Innocent-Marie was the epitome of love. He cared for all of the young men under his care and quickly became a father figure to me. The community relied heavily on him, and he had numerous responsibilities to attend to. My room was next to his, and I could hear him up late at night, long after lights-out, dictating letters into a tape recorder that he would then give to an elderly woman in the parish to type. Yet he was up first thing in the morning with everyone else. And we were up very, very early.

Father Hawker stayed in the guesthouse for a week while I got settled. Being able to see a familiar face made the transition significantly easier. I felt at ease and settled into a routine that was strict and set.

- 3:45 a.m.: Wake up (even earlier than at boot camp). One of the brothers would walk through the halls of the dormitory every morning, ringing a cowbell. We washed, got dressed, and were ready for the day.
- 4:00 a.m.: Community prayers. The priests and student brothers would go to the church for what we called the Office of Matins. The postulants studied and read scripture (we started with the historical books of the Old Testament) before joining the others for the Office of Lauds, which was followed by a thirty-minute meditation period.
- 6:30 a.m.: Breakfast, if you weren't going to a private Mass.
- 7:00 a.m.: More classes and a study session.
- 9:00 a.m.: The Office of Tierce followed by the community Mass.
- 10:30 a.m.: More classes and a study session.
- 12:00 p.m.: Community prayers (the Office of Sext) in the church followed by lunch. This was the main meal of the day.
- 1:00 p.m.: Recreation. We'd go outside for a walk in the forest. While we were allowed to speak during class, this was the one time during the day when we were free to socialize and carry on conversation. This was true for everyone, not just the postulants. The bell would ring, and we'd return to our rooms to study or take a nap.

- 2:00 p.m.–4:30 p.m.: More classes.
- 5:00 p.m.: The Office of the Vespers (evening prayers).
- 6:00 p.m.: A light dinner.
- 7:00 p.m.: Chapter meeting. The brothers gathered to update us on any news and deliver a final lesson of the day. If anyone had done anything to the community, they would publicly confess. These were all small infractions, such as breaking a dish or anything that might have made more work for a member of the community.
- 7:20 p.m.: Night prayer (the Office of Compline).
- 7:45 p.m.: Half-hour meditation before returning to our rooms.
- 8:30 p.m.: Lights-out.

I was immediately presented with a challenge: I couldn't speak French. If I couldn't speak the language, I couldn't learn anything in class. Father Innocent-Marie arranged French lessons for me. One of the parishioners trained foreign diplomats to speak French until she went on maternity leave, so I would learn from her. I'd ride a bicycle down through the countryside over to her quaint little house for lessons. We worked together five days a week for a few hours a day, usually during the study period before lunch.

One set of French lessons apparently wasn't enough, so I also began taking lessons from an elderly woman named Mademoiselle Vaquet. She was a retired French literature professor who taught me French from a literary perspective. Every day, I would get homework. Our primary text was *Les Lettres de mon Moulin* by Alphonse Daudet, and that's what I worked on during my study periods. I made early progress, but soon hit a wall as the taxing schedule began to take its toll.

I was used to moving around and starting over in new places, but the monastery was a culture shock. Everything was *so* different. Aside from the naps in the afternoon (that part I had down cold), it was difficult to adjust to the routine. I've always been a night owl, and if I wasn't working, I would sleep until 10:00 a.m., so the challenge began from the moment I woke up. I was exhausted and had trouble concentrating during the early-morning study and prayer sessions. That sometimes set the tone for the day, and I could never bounce back.

Three months into my stay, I grew homesick. I began to question what I was doing there. The weather was getting warmer, and with no air-conditioning, I had to leave the window open. At night, I could hear music playing in the distance and the sound of backyard parties. I had no idea where it was coming from or what those people were doing, but it sounded like they were having fun. I wanted to go there, see what was happening, and spend just one night enjoying myself.

That went on for a few nights, and then I stopped. I reminded myself of why I was there. I reviewed the poor decisions I had made—how I indulged in pleasure and ran away from God. How that made me feel so disappointed in myself and alone at times. I didn't want to go back to feeling that again, so I made a promise to myself. I wasn't going to quit. I was going to see this through. I would remain at the monastery until God told me I was not supposed to be there.

I took a private vow: "God, I'm not leaving here unless You tell me to go. Otherwise, I'm staying until You make it crystal clear that I should leave."

That vow is what helped me to settle down and take it one day at a time. I no longer focused on the rest of my life; all I worried about was the day before me. For all I knew, that might be all the time I had, so I learned to relax into the day and do what needed to be done. That's an attitude I first developed in that tiny dorm room late one spring night, and it's an approach that has served me well since. Learning to frame challenges in that context was a formative turning point and one of the most beneficial changes I ever made.

Shortly after taking that vow, I settled in and adapted to the new schedule. That didn't mean everything was easy. Getting used to the food took a little more time.

Brother Bernard Marie was responsible for all cooking and meal preparation. He was from Switzerland, and he was hearing impaired but very calm. When you were in his presence, you could feel how peaceful he was. He threw himself into his work and planned meals meticulously. The monastery didn't serve meat, so every meal was vegetarian—a long-standing observance dating back to the Desert Fathers, the Benedictines, and other orders. While the restrictions didn't make for savory meals, we knew they were healthy.

But our meals were not large. Breakfast would differ depending on the time of year. Monastic Lent lasted from September 15 through Easter, and during that period, we were only allowed 50 grams of oats or 50 grams of bread for breakfast. For the rest of the year, we could have both bread and oatmeal, as well as toast and jam if we wanted.

Chasing pleasure has always been my idol. That could be sexual pleasure or seeking pleasure through food. Left to my own devices, I will spend too much time chasing pleasure, and it's something I've struggled with. I work hard not to succumb to temptation and give in. After the Marines and until I left for the monastery, I indulged. I had no qualms about eating extra dessert, so my weight had ballooned to 230 pounds by the time I arrived at the monastery. The strict diet was a change, and 50 grams of bread was not a lot of food. I was not eating much food. By Christmas, I had lost weight and was down to 165 pounds.

I wasn't concerned about the weight loss. I actually felt good and was somewhat proud of myself because I had never been that thin in my life, but the priests were worried about my health. They encouraged me to eat more, insisting that I no longer fast with the rest of the community. So, while everyone else was eating their 50 grams of bread in the morning, I was told to eat as much as I wanted. I wasn't comfortable with that. I believed everyone else was looking at me, even though they really weren't, but it certainly felt that way at the time. That made eating more food harder.

To increase the calories in my diet, we reached out to my mother and had her send me a case of single-serve peanut butter packets (peanut butter is not readily available in France). I ate a couple of containers of that with my bread to increase my caloric intake.

Over Christmas, my mom added some homemade American Christmas cookies to my care package, dying the dough to make red and green cookies. When I shared those colorful cookies with the community, the brothers were utterly confused. They had never seen cookies this color before. Some didn't even want to try them, but those who bravely stepped out of their comfort zone were pleasantly rewarded. American cookies taste very good, especially when compared to our vegetarian diet.

The most interesting culinary experience was when I traveled with a few brothers to visit a parishioner's small organic farm. The farmer grew a variety of vegetables that he sold locally, allowing people to come and pick their own. Occasionally, I would go with the lay brothers to pick vegetables. That season, the farmer had decided to grow sweet corn, an American staple. Europeans don't typically eat corn on the cob. So, when the farmer tried to sell us some, one of the brothers was confused. "Why would we want corn? That's animal feed."

The farmer explained it was American sweet corn and talked them into taking enough home so everyone in the monastery could try corn on the cob. From there, the confusion only grew.

Brother Bernard Marie didn't know how to cook corn on the cob. None of the Europeans did. So, I showed them how to cook it in boiling water, how to serve it with butter, and how to pick it up and eat it with their hands.

At the beginning of each meal, we said communal grace, followed by the reading of scripture. Everyone could begin eating during the reading, but they had to remain silent. If you wanted someone to pass the food, you gestured for it. So, there was a premium placed on looking out for your brothers to ensure everyone had what they needed at the table without talking or making a disturbance. The corn on the cob truly put this system to the test.

The European brothers had no idea how to eat corn off the cob. They saw the brothers from North America eating it with their hands and looked at them as if they were savages. They didn't know what to do with the butter; no meals had ever been served with butter. I saw some trying to use a knife and fork to saw the individual kernels off the cob so they could eat it in a more civilized manner. A few cobs slid off the plates, down the table, and onto the floor. It was a sight to behold, and it was the last time we ever served corn on the cob at the monastery.

My life had improved significantly since taking that personal vow. I may have been on the other side of the globe, but it didn't feel as if I was far away from home. I felt slightly cut off from the rest of the world, but I was okay with that. We were focused directly on what we could influence and trusted that our prayers and efforts would help the world. We didn't spend a lot of time worrying about the news, or world events. We couldn't change that directly, but our prayers could help, even if we didn't "see" the change.

Although I may not have been allowed to speak freely with the other postulants and novices for more than half an hour a day, I was getting a much better feel for what was being taught in classes. After taking consistent French lessons, I was told the only time I was allowed to speak English was during confession. It took a little while longer, but I reached a point where I could confess in French.

Due to the immersion process, I was able to pick up the language much more quickly than some of the other young men who had already studied French. When they arrived, I could see the wheels turning in their heads as they translated French to English and formulated a response. I not only learned how to communicate in French (not just translate), but I also started to think and eventually dream in French. And while I'm not the best at translating French, I can pick up a book written in French, read it, and understand what it says. Even after time away, the language comes back very quickly.

I wasn't the only one who felt I was more comfortable in my new role. In September 1999, eight months into my stay, Father Innocent-Marie informed me that I would be taking the habit during a ceremony to become a novice. I had finally reached the first milestone.

The receiving of the habit was a significant event in the community, and I had been eagerly anticipating it for weeks. None of the other postulants had received the habit during my stay, so I had never attended the ceremony before. This was a big step, and I was excited. I was told I could invite friends and family, so I called my dad. He took a week off from work and traveled to France for the ceremony.

On the morning of the ceremony, the entire community of twenty-five to thirty brothers gathered inside the church. I was the last to file inside, still dressed in my postulant cape. The Mass began, and when Father Innocent Marie called me up to the altar. I walked up and lay face down on the red clay tile floor, a sign of obedience and submission to God.

Upon standing, I was escorted into the chapter room, where we gathered every day for meetings. Once I was inside, they took off my civilian clothes and put on the white robe and black cape. Friars are to wear the black cape whenever they leave the monastery or when the bishop is in residence. Otherwise, the black cape is optional.

I was escorted back toward the altar where the brothers were waiting in line for what was called "the kiss of peace." One by one, I put both hands on each of my brothers' shoulders; each brother then placed his hands on top of mine and we embraced for a chaste hug before touching our foreheads together.

Then we returned to our places for the community Mass.

Once I left the church, I was given a haircut by one of my brothers, so I had a tonsure, just like everyone else. It was a rite of passage, similar to my buzz cut at boot camp.

I was a member of the community, and that brought a sense of belonging. Previously, I had felt like the ugly duckling. Everyone else had their habit, they had settled in, they knew they would be there for a while. I didn't know how long I'd be staying or if I would even be invited to wear the habit and become a novice. I had been filled with doubt and uncertainty, but once I walked out of the church wearing the habit, all of that disappeared. All of my work and sacrifice had not been a waste. The brothers had committed to me, and that was confirmation that I had been moving in the right direction. The next step would be to take my temporary vows in a year's time. I knew that if I could do this for a year, I could do it for the rest of my life. I just had to take it one day at a time.

Once you become a novice and take the habit, the brothers give you a new name. They don't pick the usual suspects but opt for the more obscure examples. The brothers bestowed upon me the name Brother Antoine Marie. Saint Antoine Neyrot had been a Dominican brother who was captured by the Muslims in North Africa. He committed apostasy, abandoned his faith, and took a mistress, only to have a change of heart. He repented and confessed his sins. However, Muslim law doesn't allow you to leave the Islamic faith after you've converted. The penalty for that is death. The sultan whom he had pledged to serve offered Saint Antoine the choice of returning to Islam with even more wives and money or death. He chose to keep the Catholic faith and forgo the pleasures offered to him and was stoned to death. I found Brother Antoine Marie to be an interesting choice for my new name. I'm sure the brothers realized that I struggled with an inordinate attachment to the pleasures of the world, but they never explained why they chose that name for me.

Meanwhile, my dad was undergoing his own transformation, so the experience was good for him as well. I'm glad that he was able to witness something that few in the world ever get to see. He stayed in the guesthouse and was invited into the community to share a meal with us. My dad is very much a steak-and-potatoes kind of guy. He'll take meat with a side of meat whenever possible, so he didn't really know what to make of the vegetarian menu. The first night, he didn't eat much. As was the custom, he would take all of his other meals in the guesthouse. The cook would send over what everyone else was eating so the guests could eat in a more casual setting.

After a few days, the novice master pulled me aside and asked, "Is your dad okay? He doesn't seem to be eating."

"Are you serving him any meat?" I asked.

"No. Should we?"

"He does like meat."

"How about chicken? Does he like chicken?"

"I'm sure he would love chicken."

Somehow, they managed to procure a whole roast chicken for his next meal, and he devoured the entire thing in minutes. The brothers thought that was hilarious.

During my dad's visit, I was able to borrow a car for a day trip so the two of us could see Chartres Cathedral in the French countryside. We then spent two days in Paris and stayed with Father Innocent-Marie's parents overnight.

We arrived early on a Sunday morning in Paris, going to Mass at Saint-Nicolas du Chardonnet, an SSPX church in the heart of the city. Then we visited the Sainte-Chapelle and Notre-Dame. Because I was a brother, I was wearing my habit, and they permitted us to enter the treasury, which wasn't open to the public. We were able to view the overwhelming collection of holy relics on display.

As an ironworker, my dad asked to see one of the most famous and exquisite pieces of ironwork—the Eiffel Tower. It turned out to be a much farther walk than we realized, but we made it. It was my first time viewing the impressive landmark. Some said there was a consecrated Host buried under each leg of the tower, while others claimed it was designed to be taller than the tallest structures at the time (all of which were churches) in an effort to show the superiority of the Enlightenment and Revolutionary ideals. I hadn't realized there was so much anti-Catholic sentiment or myth around the Eiffel Tower. And we got quite a few strange looks as we went up the tower, but the view was stunning.

I needed to return to the Saint-Nicolas du Chardonnet for Vespers that evening, but neither of us knew how to take the bus or a cab, so we half-sprinted and half-walked across the streets of Paris and along the banks of the Seine. It was the middle of summer, and the city was sweltering. My dad was trying to run in cowboy boots; I was covered from head to toe in heavy wool. Between my habit, scapular, and cape, I was carrying an extra twenty pounds of wool.

Out of breath, my father stopped and sat on a nearby step. "Just go ahead. Leave me. I'll be okay," he gasped.

My dad didn't speak a lick of French. Obviously, I couldn't leave him alone and on the verge of a heart attack in Paris. We sucked it up and made it the rest of the way back together to Saint-Nicolas du Chardonnet, arriving just as Vespers were about to begin. My dad sat in the back of the church, and I got roped into the pool of clergy.

Vespers begins with an opening prayer, followed by an opening hymn and then five psalms. It was performed differently in the Roman liturgy than it was in the Dominican liturgy, which I had been used to. The master of ceremonies brought the main office book (a partial breviary with the musical notations) to a different cleric at the beginning of each psalm to intone the antiphon. Suddenly, on the fourth psalm, the emcee brought the office over to me to sing. I was caught off guard, and my heart jumped up in my throat. I could hardly breathe! Standing in front of all these priests and brothers and a hundred faithful in the church, I somehow managed to call upon my choir training and croaked out the intonation. It probably sounded better to everyone else than it did to me, and I'm sure they didn't notice anything amiss.

After Mass, my father and I returned to Father Innocent-Marie's parents' house for a wonderful meal with multiple courses and plenty to eat and drink. Our hosts went all out to make sure we had a nice experience. We were served anise aperitifs, cornichons and jambon avec beurre (ham with cold butter), beefsteaks, and finally chocolate éclairs. The meal was accompanied by fine French wines. By the end, both my father and I were exhausted. We woke up early the next morning and headed back to the monastery.

My dad's trip was not without incident. People drive fast in France. On the drive home from visiting one of the cathedrals, we were going 130 kph (100 mph) on a four-lane highway. Over the next kilometer, all four lanes merged into a single lane. While trying to merge, I clipped a safety cone and broke the side mirror of the car. At the next chapter meeting, I kneeled in front of the community. Holding on to a shard of the car mirror, I confessed publicly to having broken it—quite the humbling experience.

When you become a novice, you have a choice between two paths—you can become a priest or a lay brother. To become a priest, you continue to take courses and follow a different educational track than a lay brother, who performs work to help sustain the monastery, such as cooking, cleaning, and maintenance. I chose the priesthood track. Given the class load and what I was already learning as a postulant, my routine didn't change much.

The most significant change that occurred after taking the habit was that I got to see more of the French countryside and neighboring villages. I was the only novice with a driver's license. Father Innocent-Marie had arranged for me to obtain a French driver's license, which allowed me to drive him to visit people in the community and nearby religious institutions. (Apparently, my having broken the side mirror didn't deter him from riding in a car with me.)

Whenever we set out to drive, I rarely knew where we were headed. He'd direct me as we drove. "Take a left here and then a right up there." When we arrived at our destination, I was told to wait in the car. And these weren't short waits either; sometimes, I'd be waiting for two hours or more. I'd find the local church to pray and walk around the village. I learned early on that it was a good idea to bring a book. Other times, I laid down in the back seat to take a nap.

During one of these trips, Father Innocent-Marie took us to the city of Tours, France, to visit the home of Father De La Tour. He was an SSPX priest who was on sabbatical after becoming stressed and burned out from serving parishes around the world for decades. He had returned home to live with his parents in Tours. It often doesn't end well for priests who return home, because they lack religious support and that makes it difficult to reintegrate into their communities. When priests struggle, it's better they live at a retreat house or monastery, where they can be at peace with God without having to worry about worldly influences and family ties. The day of our visit, Father Innocent-Marie was able to persuade Father De La Tour to return with us to the monastery.

The De La Tour family house was over five hundred years old and was in the middle of a twenty-five-year-long renovation to modernize the home. Even the new houses under construction in town were built on concrete blocks and timber-framed roofs. They weren't building a house to last fifty years; they were building homes to last two hundred years. The way they viewed time and culture was different from what I was used to in America, where everything was immediate and involved more short-term thinking. I was invited inside to share a meal with the family. It's where I learned that when someone offers you a steak in France, unless you like it well done and tough, it's best to pass.

On our trips, we'd drive through small towns and villages that were hundreds of years old. There was hardly a distinction between the church and town. The church was the center of the town, and the houses were clustered around it in small groups. Where I came from, the community was more fractured; some of the churches weren't closely tied to the town community at all. After all, we had to fly in priests from other parts of the country.

On another trip, Father Innocent-Marie united me with my old friend Paul Torcel from the religious house in Los Gatos, California. Paul had arrived at St. Aloysius from Buffalo to explore his vocation before I left. He joined the SSPX and was accepted to attend one of their seminaries in Flavigny, France. On February 2, 2000, Father Innocent-Marie and I traveled to the monastery in Flavigny for the Feast of the Purification of the Blessed Virgin Mary. In the seminary, that is the milestone day for new postulants to receive their habits and become novices. And that's where I ran into Paul, who was receiving his habit that day. We reconnected after the ceremony, and I told him how I liked living the Dominican life. Months later, Paul would leave the SSPX to join our Dominican monastery. And he's still there today. Maybe me telling him how great it was to be a Dominican had some influence on that decision.

Every few months, Father Innocent-Marie would take small groups on longer trips, typically with another brother and a few novices. We'd take one of the cars or the small passenger van and stay at another monastery or with a parishioner from the communities we visited. It opened most of us up to a brand-new cultural experience. We were even allowed to speak more than we normally would, but every so often, the brothers would call for quiet.

On one memorable trip, we accompanied Father Innocent-Marie to the hot springs in the Pyrenees where he underwent medical treatment. While we didn't visit the actual hot springs, we did get to experience the region and the churches throughout the countryside.

What most people don't realize is that friars have traditionally relied on begging as a means of support. That's why they stay at other monasteries and with parishioners. They don't pay for hotels or lodging, and they typically don't pay for food. They bring food, and when that runs out, they turn to the community for support.

During our trip to Rome, we planned to meet up with other groups of friars and faithful from all over Europe to partake in the

Jubilee year celebrations. I was in charge of going into the city and begging for food. Not speaking the language, it was difficult to communicate. This was not something I was particularly good at, and the food that I had procured was barely edible. Thankfully, a group of faithful from Avrille, France, who were traveling with us, pitched in to provide us with food.

Begging is not easy, and Rome wasn't the first time. During another trip to Montserrat in Spain, we stopped in Barcelona to visit a monastery that was home to a community of nuns. By the end of the week, our food supply had run low. All we had left was dark French chocolate and stale bread, so upon the novice master's suggestion, we made chocolate sandwiches.

We took these trips because Father Innocent-Marie wanted us to experience Europe and see what an integral Catholic culture could produce. America is not a Catholic culture. Many of those who identify as Catholic don't attend Mass every Sunday or believe what the Church teaches. There is not a shared belief in the Catholic faith in America. Many of our founding principles have been condemned by the Catholic Church, and there has been much anti-Catholic sentiment throughout our history. But in Europe, the roots of faith ran deep.

We once visited a church in a small town where, during the French Revolution, hundreds of people were killed for being Catholic—men, women, children, and nuns. Father Innocent-Marie wanted us to see how, not long ago, people like us sacrificed their lives to remain faithful to the Church. He wanted to show us the locations where battles were fought in defense of the Church, a rich history that went back hundreds of years. That's a perspective many Americans like me didn't have. Our country is approaching its 250th anniversary, a relatively short time compared to the longevity of some other countries. The people in France and in other countries throughout Europe take pride in their country's rich history; they don't view themselves as descendants of other countries. They had a much different sensibility than Americans, and that couldn't help but influence my perspective. And, in spite of all that, I'm still proud to be an American.

The most significant change that occurred after taking the habit was spiritual, specifically the battle I had been facing with my demons over the years.

Throughout my life, when I went to sleep, I would wake up forty minutes later half-conscious and filled with a compulsive sexual urge. I had little control over that. Shortly after receiving my habit, I woke up just as I typically would, but this time, I felt what could best be described as an evil presence in my room. I couldn't see it, but intense fear pulsed through my body. There was a weight on my chest. It was difficult to breathe. The air around me felt as if it had been sucked out of the room and replaced with a foreign entity that was trying to take something from me. I've had other spiritual experiences, but none where I felt an evil presence looming over me.

I believe there are forces that influence us beyond what we can see with the naked eye. There's good and evil. God and angels are very real, as are their evil counterparts. Whether you call them demons, devils, or fallen angels, they don't want you to succeed, and they don't want what's good for you. We don't always perceive these outside forces, but I believe they do exist, and I believe that is what I encountered that night.

It's not a coincidence that the spirit visited me after I received the habit. I had been working hard to overcome those urges and change the destructive pattern I had struggled with for most of my life. This evil spirit was trying to crush that moment to prevent change. It was trying to lure me back.

The experience only lasted a minute. I don't remember the prayer I said, but it was along the lines of "I don't belong to you. I'm not yours. Jesus, help me!" In that prayer was my belief that I belonged to God. It was me calling for divine help. And then, the spirit was gone, and I was once again alone in the room.

Sweating and out of breath, I remained still for the next several minutes, trying to wrap my head around what I had experienced. It took me a long time to fall back asleep, and when I did, I slept through the night. I woke up with an overwhelming feeling of peace, one that I had not experienced in a long time. When I told Father Innocent-Marie about my experience the next day, he seemed almost excited. "Oh, you should have come and got me. It would have been an excellent time for us to pray together."

Being able to turn away from evil that night and confirming that I didn't belong to it left me with a deep sense of peace that lasted for months. It set me on a path that further confirmed my purpose and my pursuit.

As I approached my first year as a novice and eighteen total months at the monastery, I looked forward to taking my vows. I spoke to Father Innocent-Marie about this topic, assuring him I was ready to move forward and work in earnest. He insisted on beginning a twelve-week discernment program where I would pray, meditate, study, and ponder the decision. After that period, I felt that I was ready; I just needed the approval of the brothers.

When I met with Father Innocent-Marie in his room to discuss my future, I immediately sensed that the response would not be positive. I believed that I was ready to take my vows, but clearly he did not. He was very matter-of-fact about it. "It's the opinion of the brothers that you should go home."

I was devastated. I had been working so hard, everything building toward this moment, and he thought it was best that I return home. I had to ask him to repeat himself because I thought I had misunderstood him. I didn't.

"You have construction experience, right? I feel like you should go home and do that. I think it would be good for you."

"Wait a minute," I protested. "I want to take my vows. I want to move forward."

"I'm sorry, but you can't. It's been decided."

That was a moment of immense confusion. How do I pray for weeks and come to the opposite conclusion as them? I was genuinely upset at the system. It wasn't always like this. Hundreds of years ago, if you made it a year as a novice, you could take your vows. But this changed during the twentieth century when the Church felt that brothers needed to take temporary vows before permanent vows—a process that involved the novice master receiving a sign from God, which could take up to ten years. I wasn't the only novice who was frustrated, and many devout people of faith left the monastery because of this system. It shouldn't take that long to determine if God wants someone to remain. It was a foolish process.

While considering these arguments and spiraling, I remembered the promise I had made to myself fifteen months earlier: I would remain at the monastery unless I received a crystal-clear sign to leave. The brothers were in charge. They had final say. If they were telling me to leave, it couldn't get any clearer, so that was my sign. I still didn't like it or agree with the decision, but once I viewed it in that light, I could be at peace with it.

Until that point, I had a long history of quitting. I quit college. I quit the ROTC. I didn't quit the Marines, but I didn't make it through boot camp. I tried to turn over a new leaf at the religious house and again in Post Falls, Idaho, but didn't last long in either place. I had started many things that I never finished and that had taken its toll. It felt like every attempt at a fresh start took a little piece of me each time. My resolve had weakened, and I was starting to lose confidence. Having quit or run away before, it became easier to do it again.

After leaving the monastery, I didn't have that feeling. I knew that I had given everything I had to this pursuit. I couldn't have tried any harder. It didn't work out, and that was okay, because that's what God wanted for me. And for the first time in my life, I had proven to myself that I could persevere.

It was difficult to leave. The brothers didn't want me to tell anybody what had happened, so for the next three days, I went about my normal routine. On the third day, I flew home.

CHAPTER 7

Coming Home

PEOPLE WERE drawn to Immaculate Conception and the town of Post Falls, Idaho, by the church, the community, and the schools. It's why I first traveled there when I was thirteen and why I returned eight years later after boot camp. It's also what inspired my dad and Ria to move there. Their family was growing, they now had nine children of their own, so they wanted to settle down in a community with a good Catholic school system.

When I left the monastery in the fall of 2000, I moved back in with my dad and Ria in their new home in Post Falls. They were glad to see that I was healthy and well, but slightly disappointed that I had been told to return home. Meanwhile, they had settled into a fairly large but older house set on ten acres. There was a wide-open living room and a big bonus room above the garage that they had turned into a game room. They had a deck out back and a separate deck off to the side. My dad had enough room to create a reasonably sized workshop space. And just like back in Utah, they had a barn with a couple of horse stalls. They had also put in a round pen with sand in the backyard for the horses. After spending two years in France, this felt like a little piece of Americana.

I took over the parlor room and slept there for a short while before moving to one of the finished bedrooms in the basement. It didn't take long to adjust. Life at their home was simple. We watched sports on TV and the occasional movie, but it was very low-key and low-stress. I didn't bring any baggage or pressure with me into this new environment. It truly felt like a fresh start, and I had the chance to do what I wanted with my life. I was twenty-three years old and I knew I wanted a family, but I wasn't ready for marriage yet—at least not financially. If I wanted to take that step, I would first need a steady job, and by this point in my life, I was most qualified to work in the construction industry.

My dad had purchased a 1991 Chevy short-bed truck with a canopy from a priest named Patrick Crane. It had a lot of miles on it, but Father Crane knew my dad was broke and had kids, so he gave him a good deal. When I moved back, my dad sold me the truck at a price I thought was fair. I later learned from Ria that he sold it to me for more than he paid for it. Thanks, Dad!

I hadn't been home long before I started getting regular iron-work jobs—rebar, welding, and decking work. After six months, I had a little money in my pocket. I was able to move out and found a small, one-bedroom, one-bathroom house to rent, just a block from the church, for $400 a month. Oddly enough, my old roommate Jerry Wade—the class clown and life of the party—was also looking for a place to stay. He had never led me into trouble, so he moved in, and we lived there together.

I had been home for a few months when I joined the youth group at Immaculate Conception. It was more of a social club and learning environment for young adults. There were approximately twenty-five people between the ages of eighteen and twenty-eight who got together to take trips, including hiking, canoeing, and biking. We played a lot of Ultimate Frisbee in the summer and took snowshoeing trips during the winter. There was a learning component to it, but it wasn't as formal as Sunday school. We would gather to watch presentations on church history or scripture. Sometimes, the lessons would be about art or music related to the church. It was a way to bring young people in the community together, allowing them to learn more about the faith and the formation of the church while engaging in fun activities. The group did have strict rules. Members had to be out of high school and unmarried. Some of the coed youth groups in the area turned into dating pools, so it was a rule that members couldn't date anyone in the group. If you did date another member, one of you had to leave the group.

In the summer of 2001, Father Morgan, who had replaced Father Boyle, recruited me to become the president of the group. This involved putting together the group agenda with Father Morgan, teaching the lessons, and organizing the group activities. I dove in headfirst and had fun with it. That helped to give me a bit more stability and direction. And then, in the fall of 2001, everything changed.

After Mass on Sunday, I went to the grocery store. That's where I saw the woman I was going to marry. *That's the one!* I didn't know her name, and I had never met her before, but I just knew it. That feeling—the one that started in my gut and rushed throughout my body—was what made me so certain. With her bright brown eyes and thick, curly brown hair that fell past her shoulders, this woman pushed all the right buttons for me. She was slim and modest in dress and comportment. I was drawn to her musical laugh, but it was the way that she radiated joy and a naive innocence that made her the perfect match. Even at twenty-one, she had the freshness of youth. There was a purity and brightness to her that immediately drew me.

Her name was Gina McQuade, and she was the younger sister of Jerry, Dennis, and Pat—three brothers, all in their early twenties, whom I had recruited to join the church youth group. I hadn't seen Gina at church before, but that wasn't unusual. I was singing in the Schola at the front of the church, up in the sanctuary. My focus was on the altar, not the crowd. She could have been there every week, and I wouldn't have seen her. There were many people in the community I had never met before.

I didn't talk to Gina that day, but I later talked to her brothers about inviting her to the youth group. She came to one function, but she was busy teaching at a small private Catholic school and took the work seriously, correcting homework and planning lessons.

Gina's family lived on a five-hundred-acre homestead near Marble Creek, about eighty miles from the church. Given the location, it was a two-hour drive from Post Falls, so attending church and participating in the youth group was a significant commitment for the family. Numerous cabins and trailers were spread throughout their property, which was right on the water. They had one of the only sandy beaches located on the St. Joe River. The brothers were all outdoors types. They had grown up in the mountains and had spent their entire lives in the country. They hunted, distilled their own whisky, and made their own wine.

I had been dating other girls I wasn't very attracted to. Part of me felt that's what I deserved. I had ugliness inside me, and these relationships were a match made in the mud pit. When I told Father Hawker, he was shocked, "What are you talking about? You absolutely need to be attracted to the person you're going to marry. Don't be foolish. You have to live with this person. They won't become any more attractive. Imagine how you'll think of them in twenty years." Of course, he was right. I guess that's why he was the priest.

Something was changing within me. I wanted to settle down, get married, and have kids. That required more than attraction. For me, being a good Catholic parent meant wanting to have the children God sent you and educating them in the fullest sense of the word. They needed basic education and training in virtue, and most importantly they needed to be taught their faith, not just by memorizing or following rules, but deep in their hearts. There is a special way in which moms impart faith with every drop of milk and food that soaks in and fosters a sense of wonder and joy in their children. I saw the work Gina was doing educating kids, and I realized she would be in alignment with me when it came to children.

She would impart the faith to her children in a way that only a mother could. That's what I sought in my partner.

One Saturday, my dad, a few of my siblings, and I drove to Gina's family homestead to harvest firewood. While we were there, Pat, Dennis, and Jerry agreed to help. We ventured up the hill and into the woods looking for some good trees. We cut them down, split the wood, and made our way back down the hill with firewood to load into everyone's trucks. What I didn't realize was that Gina's brothers were watching me closely to see what kind of worker I was. Was I a city slicker, or could I actually wield an axe? I wasn't an experienced outdoorsman like the McQuade brothers, but this wasn't my first time cutting firewood either. We grew up with a woodstove in our home, so I had split plenty of firewood as a kid. That day helped me earn the brothers' seal of approval. At the very least, they didn't think I was a chump.

I started spending more and more time at the homestead with Gina's brothers. When there, I'd stay in her brother Jerry's boot shop on the property. He had gone to school to learn how to make boots and leather goods, so he set up his little shop on the property. I would stay down there and we'd drink cheap beer. When with the family, we played a lot of pinochle and I'd shoot guns with the brothers in the mountains. During the winter, we'd find patches of icicles in the distance and see who could shoot them out. Turns out I'm not a bad shot with my old Remington Fieldmaster.

When out on the property, it wasn't uncommon to have a run-in with the occasional moose. They'd eat the shrubs and destroy all the trees. They were also fearless animals who hated the world, so we tried to chase them off whenever they ventured too close. One morning, when I was staying at the boot shop, Jerry woke me up to help chase away a moose. He had a tiny flare gun and told me to grab something. By that, I'm sure he meant a pistol, but I didn't have a gun, so I grabbed the only thing I had in my car, which was a three-foot-long steel pry bar. I have no idea why I thought I could defend myself from a moose with a pry bar, and luckily, I didn't have to find out. We managed to chase the moose up the river and away from the homestead by shooting flares.

Between 2001 and 2002, I became really good friends with all of Gina's brothers. Having bounced around between different schools as a kid and forced to socially maneuver in between various friend groups, I had a knack for learning how to fit in. In a way, this was like school all over again—like putting on a new outfit. I showed that I could work in the woods and live in their world. It wasn't a stretch, and I loved hanging out with all the brothers, but primarily, I was driving two hours up there so I could be close to Gina.

Gina and I weren't dating yet, but by December 2001, I was so certain that she was the one that I went to the local jewelry store to buy a diamond for the engagement ring. I knew the rule of thumb was one month's salary, which was $1,600 (and a lot of money for me back in the day), so I wanted to start paying for it early. The diamond remained with the jeweler, and I slowly paid for it over time. The only person I told was Father Hawker. In case it didn't pan out, I wanted to keep these plans to myself.

Gina wasn't stupid. She knew I was interested. I think she was being coy and playing hard to get. But to be fair, she had also been thinking about joining the convent. So, there was never a moment when we officially started dating. It was a gradual progression, but by the summer of 2002, roughly six months after our first meeting, it was clear we were a couple. I decided to leave the youth group and resign as president. They had a strict no-dating policy, and I was on the path to marriage. I wanted to be responsible and respect the group's rules.

What made dating and getting to know Gina so difficult was that I had to spend long stretches away from home because of work. In spring, I took a job working at Boeing Field in Renton, Washington, which is located near Seattle. That was a four-and-a-half-hour drive from Post Falls. It's not an ideal situation, but when working construction in the Pacific Northwest, you go where the work is.

I found a place to stay with two Naval officers with whom I shared a mutual friend. They lived in Kingston, Washington, which was an hour north of Renton and across Puget Sound. So, I would park my car at a church in Edmonds, Washington. I'd take the ferry across the sound to Kingston to spend the night with my friends. I'd wake up early to catch the 5:30 a.m. ferry back to Edmonds to get my car and drive an hour south to the job in Renton. The job was six days a week, ten hours a day. We got Sundays off, so when I finished work on Saturday, I'd drive four and a half hours home to hang out with Gina and her brothers before driving back to the jobsite so I could make it to work on Monday morning. I did that for five weeks.

I worked other jobs in Portland, Oregon, and Marysville, Washington. On some trips, my only contact with Gina was over the phone. This was a time when cell phone companies charged by the minute. I'd occasionally wind up with some hefty monthly bills close to $400, which was almost a week's pay.

On one job, I was installing a new antenna on the top of a five-hundred-foot radio tower. It was considered an ironworking job because it required the same safety protocols and skill sets needed to climb a steel structure. It was a short, two-day job, but one that involved free-climbing the outside face of the tower. Despite the law and what the paperwork stipulated, the gear I was given would not allow me to be secured to the structure the whole time, so this was not a job without its risks.

It was a three-man job—me, the boss, and one other guy. The first day was all prep work—that was our first trip up and down. The second day was dedicated to the installation, during which we needed to mount and secure the antenna to the top of the tower.

After making the half-hour climb to the top, we had only been working for a short while when we could see a severe thunderstorm approaching in the distance. The boss assured us, "Everything is going to be fine." When you're five hundred feet up in the air with a storm approaching and lightning in the distance (while you're secured to a metal tower), everything doesn't seem like it's going to be fine. Still, we kept working, and sure enough, we got hit by the storm. The rain poured, and the wind gusted, but we finished the job.

Climbing down the slick metal frame of the tower was not easy and took much longer than it had the day before. By the time we reached the ground, the storm had passed. When we were done for the day, the boss told us, "You guys are some of the bravest sons of bitches I ever worked with. Anybody else would have climbed down as soon as they spotted that storm on the horizon. I appreciate you."

We just looked at each other and shrugged. We didn't realize climbing down was an option. If we had, that's probably what we would have done.

That job led to another with the same company, this time climbing an 860-foot tower. For this tower, we could hook into an industrial winch that was already set up to hoist us to the top of the tower. The entire ride up, I dangled off the ground from a thin wire rope with nothing below. Carnival rides were not nearly as exciting after that experience.

Soon, I had enough money to pay for the ring. But I still wasn't sure if Gina would accept my proposal. We got along and had fun together, but I didn't know if she felt ready for marriage. There was only one way to find out.

Gina's parents liked me—at least, I believe they did. It was difficult to tell. Her father, Thomas, was a crusty old curmudgeon who didn't have a lot to say. He was seventy-two at the time; he had married and had children late in life and was twenty years older than his wife. We got along well enough. Gina's mom, Karen, liked me because I carried myself well. I didn't put much emphasis on appearances, but I made sure to dress well—slacks and nice shoes. I was also willing to pray with the family. I attended Mass and had a good job. It didn't hurt that I had also lived in the monastery. All of that helped make a good impression on Gina's mom at least.

In anticipation of my proposal, I first asked permission from her father. I was at the homestead, and I waited until her brothers had left for church in the afternoon so the two of us would be alone. It was the perfect opportunity for some one-on-one time to discuss the future. He was in the living room, sitting in his La-Z-Boy watching PBS—that was always more background than anything else. I sat next to him in Grandma's chair, and for the longest time, we didn't say anything. Finally, I broke the silence. "Mr. McQuade, I'd like to talk with you about taking your daughter's hand in marriage."

"What?" He was startled.

"I'd like to marry your daughter."

There was a long silence that left me more concerned by the second. I hadn't been looking forward to this conversation, and he wasn't making it particularly easy for me to get comfortable. Finally, he furrowed his brow and said, "What the hell would you want to do that for?"

That was not the answer I expected to hear.

"Because I love your daughter," I told him.

There was another long, tense silence before he said, "Good luck getting any work out of her. But if that's what you want to do, then fine."

I never could have predicted that response, but it wasn't a no. And that was all I needed to hear. And in July 2002, I decided to propose.

Gina and her sister Roseanne had come to town, and Roseanne was chaperoning as Gina and I took a walk through nearby Falls Park. I asked Roseanne if I could have some time alone with Gina. When Roseanne disappeared down a side trail, Gina and I rounded a bend and were alone near a rock outcropping. That's when I got down on one knee. I now know that whenever I ask Gina a question, there is often a long pause, and that was what happened then.

The conversation with her father was nerve-racking, but this silence was ten times worse because I was not sure what she would say.

I put the ring on her finger, and she looked at me in confusion. "What does this mean?"

"I'm asking you to marry me."

"Then why are you putting the ring on my right hand?"

Awesome. Well, we were off to a great start. I wasn't sure what would happen. I knew Gina loved me. I also knew she had been considering the convent. The fact that I was a Catholic was important, because Gina had watched one of her sisters struggle to keep the faith after marrying a non-Catholic. I was someone who wanted to raise a Catholic family and live a healthy lifestyle. Her spiritual adviser knew the situation. He saw that she had a good man with a good job who wanted to get married, and he knew that she wanted a family, so he encouraged the positive decision.

About a week after I proposed, Gina finally said yes and agreed to get married, but she didn't want to rush it. We were working on a budget, and she took preparation seriously. She had saved money and didn't want to burden her parents with the cost of a wedding. Having spent a lot of time taking care of her older sisters' twins, Gina wanted to do things the right way. There are times in the Catholic church calendar when you don't want to get married, such as during Advent and Lent. Typically, you wait a week or two after Easter. Gina was teaching school and wanted to finish the year before focusing on the wedding, so the date we picked was May 10, 2003.

In the meantime, Gina and I searched for a place to live once we were married. I had steady work and was back on my feet. I had also inherited $10,000 from my maternal grandfather after he passed away while I was at the monastery in France. (My mom had kept it from me because she didn't want the money to go to the monastery. Once I returned and she saw that I was engaged and planning to start a family, she told me what had happened and sent me a check.)

During our search, I asked Gina what she needed in a new home. She said, "Running water and electricity."

"Other than that, you don't care?" I asked.

"As long as it has running water and electricity, I'll be fine."

That was as straightforward as it gets.

The house we found wasn't really a house so much as it was a single-wide trailer with an addition on one side. It was set on three acres with so many trees that it felt like a park. The seller was asking $75,000, but I was able to negotiate it down to $65,000 given its condition, which included a dirt floor in the addition. (We still joke about our first home having a dirt floor.) But that dirt floor meant the lender considered it raw land, which required a 30 percent down payment. Between the money I had saved and the inheritance, I was just able to afford it. I moved in while Gina continued living at the family homestead until after the wedding.

We were engaged, but we were still getting to know each other. In many ways, we were still strangers. Unfortunately, it was a tragedy that brought us closer together and resulted in one of our stronger bonding moments.

Little Eric was a sixteen-year-old family friend of the McQuade brothers. They gave him that name so as not to confuse him with their actual cousin, Eric. Little Eric lived about ten miles down the road and he came from a broken home, so the brothers took him under their wing. Little Eric soon became a member of the family, and the brothers treated him like one of their own. He was always at the homestead and even began attending church. He hadn't been baptized yet, but he was on the path to converting to Catholicism.

One day in September 2002, Little Eric went missing. He had last been seen at the homestead, so after a couple of days of not hearing from him, everyone went out to look. Eventually, they found him. He had taken out a four-wheeler and had wrecked it in the woods just off one of the main roads. His body was found pinned between the vehicle and a tree. He was dead.

Everyone who knew Little Eric was in shock. His death was a

traumatic experience for Gina and her brothers. Little Eric's mother was devastated, but she didn't have the money for a proper burial. She instructed the funeral home to make the necessary arrangements at the lowest possible cost. She wasn't Catholic, and she had just lost her son, so she arranged for him to be cremated. When Gina, her brothers, and I learned that, we stepped in. Out of respect for the dead, we wanted to bury our friend.

I went with Gina to the funeral home. It would cost an extra $2,500 to arrange for a burial, which I agreed to pay. To further complicate matters, the body hadn't been embalmed or stored for a burial. Transportation of the body would also need to be arranged, so a series of issues had to be worked out. Together with Gina and her brothers, we devised a plan.

According to Idaho law, you're allowed to transport a body inside the state to perform your own burial however you'd like. If we could provide the casket, we could transport the body to a small cemetery plot on the family homestead, about two hours away from the funeral home. One of the McQuade brothers dug the grave. I enlisted the help of a friend to make the casket. We brought the casket to the funeral home. They lowered the body inside, and we sealed it. We then loaded it into one of the brothers' pickup trucks and drove it to the cemetery plot. A priest from Immaculate Conception came with us. Once at the cemetery, the priest performed the funeral rites. We lowered the casket into the ground and took turns shoveling dirt into the grave until it was completely filled.

It was a heartbreaking experience for Gina and her family. Despite the circumstances, we did the legwork and made some difficult decisions to provide what we believed Little Eric deserved. That tragedy brought us closer together.

Being with Gina helped me to settle down. After years of wandering, it finally felt like I was home. I was no longer running, but moving in the direction God wanted me to go. I had found the woman I loved, and we were getting married for what we believed to be the right reasons, according to the Church. I was on an upward trajectory and growing in my relationship with God. Life wasn't perfect, but I couldn't have asked for more.

CHAPTER 8

Building a Foundation

THE FAMILY is a sacred institution. The Catholic Church believes that the family is critical to the well-being of society. Therefore, they go to great lengths to protect the family. It's why divorce is frowned upon. Marriage is a sacrament, an unbreakable union that comes with responsibility.

Like every couple considering marriage, Gina and I underwent a series of background checks by the Church to determine if we had been baptized and confirmed and to learn if we had ever been married before. They wanted to ensure that we were genuinely committed to getting married and that neither of us were pressured or coerced into the union. They were looking for anything that could be cause for annulment down the road.

We were then encouraged to receive training. We attended classes run by Father Crane (the priest whose truck I had been driving for a year after returning from France) intended to teach young couples what it meant to be married, the roles of husband and wife, spousal responsibilities, and obligations to their children. They wanted young couples to better understand, at least to some extent, what they were getting themselves into. More importantly, they wanted marriages to succeed and have the best possible outcome for the children.

After the classes (which took approximately eight weeks) Father Crane recommended a formal betrothal ceremony, which is a premarriage commitment. It required both of us to solemnly promise God that we would enter into the union together unless some significant outside forces intervened. After we completed that ceremony, I felt an overwhelming sense of relief. *She can't back out unless something crazy happens.* I could sit back and count the days until we got married.

Gina and I had arranged for a high Mass at the church, which was a more elaborate Mass than the typical Sunday service, with portions of the liturgy sung by the Schola. We weren't working with a big budget. We only had $5,000 to cover everything, so we coordinated with the church florist to have the Sunday-morning flowers brought in early. This way, the church's flowers for the week could also serve as our wedding flowers at the altar—and they made sure the flowers were white. Uncle Jack—not really anyone's uncle, just a family friend—had some high-end camera gear, so his gift to us was to serve as the wedding photographer.

I know the husband is not supposed to see the bride in the wedding dress before the ceremony, but I helped Gina shop for a wedding gown. We couldn't afford a new dress, so we found a nice preowned silk dress that she liked, which was very modest. We took it to a seamstress and had it modified so it fit perfectly. Everything was falling into place, but those final days leading up to the wedding weren't without drama.

Members of my extended family wanted to throw Gina a bridal shower. Grandpa Des and Grandma Mitze had moved from California to Idaho and were living next to my dad and Ria. That's where they decided to host the shower. It was a typical bridal shower; they played games and handed out gifts. When Gina opened a gift, she showed it to the group.

Everything was going well until it was time to open Grandma

Mitze's gift. Gina is very conservative and shy, so when she opened the box and saw lingerie inside, she slammed the lid shut, said "Thank you," and put the box down.

My grandmother said, "You need to show everybody what it is."

"I'm not showing everybody what that is."

"No, really. Show them."

"It's not their business."

"If you don't show everybody what's in the box, I'm not going to the wedding."

"Okay, then."

Gina didn't budge and neither did my grandmother. It was a tense moment for all.

The next day, I received a call from Grandpa Des. "Your fiancée offended and embarrassed my wife in front of the family. We're not going to the wedding unless Gina apologizes."

Of course, I was going to support my fiancée, so I told him, "Grandpa, do you know what happened? Gina doesn't want to show off lingerie for everyone to see. Grandma pushed it on her, and I don't think there is anything to apologize for. If anything, she owes Gina an apology."

"If that's your answer, and Gina won't apologize, I guess we won't be at your wedding."

That stung, but I didn't think they would follow through and not go to the wedding, so I put it out of my mind. Besides, I was busy making arrangements of my own.

Because I had lived by myself for almost a year in the trailer that Gina and I would soon share, it didn't yet have a woman's touch. When my mom flew in from Florida for the wedding and saw it, she said, "We need to make this look like a home. You can't bring your wife back into a train wreck."

On the day before the wedding, my mom took me shopping to help spruce the place up. We bought a bed for the master bedroom—or the room that would serve as the master bedroom. She helped me pick out sheets and a comforter, along with the essentials that would make the house feel more welcoming. It was one more thing off my mind.

On the morning of my wedding day, I went to the 8:30 a.m. Mass at church to pray and go to confession—polish up the old soul prior to taking this big step. That's when I saw my grandparents in church, and it hit me. If they were at the early Mass, that meant they really weren't coming to the wedding. That hurt, and it would take years to mend that relationship, but I wouldn't bring that sadness into the ceremony, so I went home to take some time for myself and get ready.

You hear stories about the bride being late to church. At our wedding, Gina was worried that *I* wouldn't show up.

Thirty minutes before the ceremony, I got a frantic call from my best man, Scott Wilson. "Are you coming? Because if you're not coming, I'll tell Gina." His voice was an octave higher than normal.

"What are you talking about? I live five minutes away. I've got plenty of time. I'm putting on my tux right now. Calm down."

"Okay, but you're coming, right? Gina's freaking out that you're not here."

None of my close friends had gotten married yet. I didn't know I had to be at the church early. Everything there was already taken care of—I had just been there that morning. There wasn't anything for me to do. Apparently, that was the wrong assumption to make. People want the groom to be there well in advance of the ceremony to stand around and be nervous.

There's a great picture on my office wall of Gina holding the corsage she made for me, with an expression of exhausted relief on her face. The photo was snapped the moment she learned I had indeed arrived at the church.

Despite the early-morning anxiety and theatrics, everything was perfect when I arrived, and the wedding began on time. We had about 125 guests fill the church. My mom made the trip from Florida where she now lived. My sister, Shawn, her husband Tim, and their son, Ryan, traveled to the wedding. Of course, my dad, Ria, and all my other brothers and sisters were there.

I heard the organ start playing as Gina's two nieces, who served as her flower girls, led the way down the aisle, throwing rose petals where they walked. Then I watched as Gina approached from the back of the church and, as I did, I was overwhelmed with joy—all the sadness from the morning vanished. Her father escorted her, wearing an old black suit and tie. (It was nice to see the crusty old logger swelling with emotion as he walked his daughter down the aisle.)

As the two made their way toward the altar, the ornate beadwork on Gina's gorgeous white silk dress twinkled under the lights, the train sweeping along the floor behind her like she was a queen. (And she still is my queen.) She's not one to wear a lot of makeup, but her face was artfully made up and practically glowed underneath her veil. Her beautifully styled hair was the perfect enhancement. She was breathtaking.

When they reached the altar, Gina knelt in front of her father to receive his blessing. He lifted the front of her veil and kissed her on the forehead, and I saw him shed a tear. When she stood, he took her hand in his and extended it to me. I accepted her hand, and we stepped together toward the sanctuary to begin the wedding ceremony.

There's a custom in some Eastern European countries where the husband and wife hold on to the same crucifix while exchanging their vows. As a tribute to Gina's Polish ancestry, we wanted to adhere to the custom. We liked the symbolism of Christ being the center or heart of our marriage. It was an acknowledgment that there would be moments of pain and suffering on the horizon, and this was a way to own that from the beginning and to serve as a reminder not to run away from the difficult times. That crucifix was going to become a focal point in our home, so we had picked out a nice one beforehand. Today, it's hanging above the bed in our master bedroom.

Those who haven't been to a traditional Catholic wedding may find it a bit confusing. Stand up. Sit down. Stand up. Kneel.

After the bride and groom enter the sanctuary, the priest gives this "tougher than you can imagine and it's not too late to run away" sermon. Then, the actual marriage takes place.

Most people think the priest marries the happy couple, but the husband and wife minister the sacrament to each other as they take their vows. The priest is only there to guide and witness the sacramental act by the couple and to record it officially with the witnesses in case the records are needed later.

Once the vows are repeated, the rings are blessed and presented to each other. No kiss.

Then it's time for the nuptial Mass. There are prayers and blessings added to the Mass that harken back to the Old Testament.

It had been an incredibly long journey for the two of us to reach this point, and there were moments when I doubted it would ever occur, but there we were, at the beginning of something wonderful and new.

After the ceremony, we had two receptions. The first was in the reception hall of the church, which was in the basement. It was a cake-and-wine reception for those who had attended the wedding. Because we were budget conscious, our cake was a gift from one of the young ladies in the youth group—a multilayer cake with white frosting and traditional embellishments as well as fresh edible flowers. The cake topper was a happy couple standing under an arch, arm in arm. Gina had made the arch and decorated it with silk flowers and beads. It was simple, elegant, and beautiful. We had fruit punch and boxed wine. Uncle Jack took pictures, and we chatted with our guests.

When it was time to go, we caught the young men who were "decorating" our truck with shaving cream and whipped cream. They had greased the door handles and tied multiple strings of cans to the driveline beneath. We made them clean up enough of the mess that we wouldn't ruin our clothes getting inside. Then, we made the two-hour drive to Gina's family homestead, where her father had built a pavilion out of raw pine logs and tarps in the pasture.

All family members who didn't make the trip to the church came to this reception—and there were well over a hundred people there. Aside from the immediate family, it was a brand-new group of people at the homestead reception. We sat down for a big potluck dinner followed by another cake. By the end of the night, everyone was exhausted. Gina and I had to stop on the way home for a nap in the truck. So much for an exciting and amorous wedding night.

For our honeymoon, we returned to France. Gina had traveled to Europe the previous spring to visit different convents and religious houses. She had even stopped by the monastery where I had lived and had met Father Innocent-Marie while visiting the nearby convent for Dominican nuns.

We flew into Paris and rented a car. Our first stop was the monastery so that Father Innocent-Marie could take part in the joy of our union. He was happy and delighted that we would come by to see him and get his blessing. We stayed at the guesthouse for two days. It felt good to be reunited with Father Innocent-Marie. Gina was impressed by the affection and paternal love he showed. After leaving the monastery, we spent the rest of the week driving through France and Switzerland before returning home to begin our new life together.

Once we were back from the honeymoon, Gina settled in and worked hard to make the trailer ours. There were still some things lacking in the home, but we put a lot of time and effort into our renovation efforts. We remodeled the addition, added wood paneling, and put in a woodstove. We had logs delivered, and I'd cut the firewood myself. I loved the location on the side of a mountain, overlooking the Rathdrum Prairie. It was particularly great on the 4th of July and at Christmastime. Despite its shortcomings, it did feel like home.

Gina and I weren't back from Europe long before we experienced another big change. It was June 2003 when I returned home from work one night to find her setting the dinner table. I immediately sensed something was off. On the table was a note with a pressed flower and contact paper. It read, "The thought of you being a daddy sends a thrill through my whole body."

Gina was pregnant.

I'm not sure what my reaction was. My emotional responses can often be somewhat delayed, but I was shocked and uncertain. It took me a long time to process what was happening. I was happy to learn that I would be a father. I was also surprised that it was happening so quickly. I had an idea in my head that Gina and I would have a year or two to enjoy the early years of getting to know each other as a couple. I was twenty-six. Was I even ready to be a father? I felt like a kid playing an adult.

I didn't grow up in an ideal environment and I wanted to be intentional about doing things differently as a parent. Most significantly, we intended to raise our children as Catholic. Faith was important to us, so we planned to take our children to church early and say family prayers together.

About two months into the pregnancy, I received another shock. We were going to have twins. *Whoa! This is going to be a bigger responsibility than I thought.* Both of Gina's older sisters had given birth to twins, so she wasn't nearly as intimidated as I was. There was nothing I could do to prepare myself, and I didn't have much time to think about it anyway. Gina started to suffer terrible morning sickness. She didn't want to take any medication, so those early days were difficult. I was occasionally traveling for work, and since Gina had stopped teaching before the wedding, she was often home alone. Everything that followed was a blur.

After researching hospital care, we learned that that many of the decisions made by hospital staff during childbirth were for the benefit of the doctors and the insurance company, rather than what was best for the mother and the child. Gina wanted to give birth at home, and I agreed. We began working closely with a pair of midwives who would help deliver the twins. In addition to working with the midwives, we also had a doctor, so if anything went wrong, there was someone there during the delivery with whom we were familiar. We had already established a relationship with the doctor when we went to get the ultrasounds. Still, we hadn't taken any prep classes with doctors because we were doing that with the midwives.

At least, that was the plan until Gina's condition devolved into preeclampsia in the fall of 2003. The situation worsened over the ensuing months.

On January 6, 2004, five weeks before her due date, the midwives were not comfortable with the situation and advised us to go to the Kootenai Medical Center in Coeur d'Alene for evaluation. We weren't panicking yet, but I was starting to feel a little nervous. It was our first pregnancy, so I was on my guard.

The friendly staff helped us get settled into a delivery room. After taking vitals and doing a brief examination, the obstetrician told us the labor wasn't advancing fast enough and, as complications mounted, he needed to induce delivery.

The doctor wanted to use a drug called Cytotec, which is very effective at causing uterine contractions, but it does so independently of all the other functions of the birth canal. This creates a defined timetable: administer Cytotec and a few minutes later—boom—labor begins. However, Cytotec tends to cause physical trauma to the mother because her body is not adequately prepared for labor. Inducing pregnancy is not the on-label use for Cytotec. It had been approved by the FDA to prevent NSAID-related ulcers; it just happened to produce predictable-onset uterine contractions as a side effect. That's why we had agreed beforehand not to use Cytotec, and that's what I told the doctors.

Instead, we allowed the doctors to administer Pitocin, which has a more random timetable. It activates the system, but it takes more time because it unfolds naturally and mimics normal birth. The doctor also wanted to administer magnesium sulfate. By this time, I was on the defensive, so I demanded more information. It took them so long to dig up the information that they never ended up using it. (Turns out magnesium sulfate is Epsom salt and reduces inflammation. It probably would have made the Pitocin more effective, but Gina wasn't going into labor fast enough.)

In the early hours of the morning, Gina underwent an emergency C-section. The procedure was a success and on January 7, 2004, we were able to briefly hold our twin boys, James and Tescelin. James was named after the Apostle James, brother of John. Tescelin was named after Saint Bernard of Clairvaux's father.

I was more in shock than anything else. I had been in survival mode for so long that I didn't have the chance to bond emotionally with my new sons, who had been born five weeks premature. After they were put under observation, the doctors administered X-rays, and that's when they saw what looked like a perforation or a faulty valve in one of the boys' hearts. If that were the case, the hospital was not equipped to handle the condition. After the diagnosis, we arranged for the twins to be baptized before they were emergency airlifted to Sacred Heart Medical Center in Spokane, Washington, where the NICU was better suited to manage the situation.

Over the next three days, I made the thirty-minute drive back and forth between the hospital in Coeur d'Alene, where Gina was recovering, and the NICU in Spokane, where the boys were being treated. It was a relief when Gina recovered and was discharged. *My wife is okay; now I can focus on the kids.*

Not long after, we learned that the boys were healthy—nothing was wrong. The boys remained in the NICU for another ten days, and then we were able to bring them home.

In the Catholic faith, you are supposed to be open to whatever life God sends you. One of the main reasons people get married is to have children. You may not get to live in a big house or drive beautiful cars, but you can have blessings in your life in the form of children who love you and depend on you. There is a lot of good to be had in the creation of the family. If you can't have children, or if there is some reason why you don't have children, that's okay.

There are other ways to contribute to the community. That was the mindset Gina and I had when we entered our marriage. We were open to having as many children as God would send us.

He didn't waste any time sending us more.

We were blessed again when Gina became pregnant in the fall of 2004. Our third son, Brendan, was delivered by the midwives in our home in May 2005 after thirty-six hours of labor. Fast-forward twenty-one months to February 2007 and my wife was nine months pregnant with our fourth son. Her due date was fast approaching, but the midwives assumed it would be another long labor. They told us to keep them posted, but wait to contact them until the contractions were relatively close together.

Gina went into labor in the middle of the night on February 19. I did my best to comfort her, and when the contractions were close enough together, I phoned the midwives.

"Check to see if the baby is coming," one of them told me.

But the baby couldn't be coming because the midwives weren't here yet.

"Really, check to see if the baby is coming." she said emphatically.

I looked. And the baby was definitely coming. Unfortunately, the midwives lived ninety minutes away. This baby was not going to wait for them. Our three sons were sound asleep in the other room. Gina and I were all alone.

Throughout human history, men have been excluded from the birth process; they tend to remain on the sidelines. Few husbands feel comfortable watching their wives give birth, and I was no exception. When Gina was in labor with Brendan, she was clearly uncomfortable, but I felt powerless to do anything about it. I was there to rub her back and hold her hand, but I couldn't solve that problem. This time, I was the only one in the room. It didn't matter if I wasn't in my comfort zone. I couldn't run away. No one else was going to catch the child. I was the one to catch him. Overcome with joy, love, relief, and an adrenaline crash, I put our baby boy in her arms.

It's amazing to watch the chemical and emotional reaction that occurs when a mother gives birth to a child. What begins as an extremely painful experience becomes one of pure joy and love once the mother holds that baby. Gina was completely absorbed in the world of our son. All I could do was cover her with a blanket and try to make her as comfortable as possible until the midwives arrived thirty minutes later.

Our family was growing bigger by the year, and I wanted to be at home with my wife and children. Unfortunately, that was not always possible. I needed to provide for them, and that still required travel, taking on small jobs one after another, with the occasional big job in between. The good news was that I was advancing in my career.

I had finished the necessary six thousand hours to take the journeyman exam. That had provided me with more options and control over the jobs I could work. It wouldn't be as much of a hustle and grind anymore, and the penalties weren't as steep if a job didn't pan out. A journeyman could travel to different jurisdictions, put their name on the list, and be considered for available union work in the area without requiring special permission from the apprenticeship department. During the early years of our marriage, I continued to expand my skill set. That created more opportunities for me, so finding work wasn't as difficult as it had been in the past—it just wasn't always close to home.

I wasn't home as often as I would have liked. And even when I was home, I don't believe I was always emotionally available. I didn't connect well with my emotions yet because I hadn't learned how to speak that language. I had briefly mentioned my childhood struggles to Gina prior to our wedding, but I didn't go into details. Society and the Church encouraged us not to burden our spouse by discussing any sexual encounters in the past because that could bring dysfunction into the relationship. Today, people take a different approach, and it's more acceptable to have that conversation with your prospective partner.

I had hoped that marriage would be the solution to the impure thoughts and sexual urges I had been struggling with for most of my life. With a wife, I believed that I would finally have the healthy outlet I needed to help me overcome what I believed to be a problem. I wish it had been that easy. Even after a few years of marriage, the struggles remained the same, and that only heightened my feelings of shame. I was convinced something was wrong with me and that it was all my fault. With nobody to talk to about any of this, I suffered in silence, and that put an unnecessary strain on our marriage. It would be many years before I understood the true nature of the problem and found the solace I sought.

No matter how difficult things got, Gina and I always remained faithful to each other. We prioritized family. Instead of trying to avoid suffering or take the easy way out, we persevered. In modern society, many people try to avoid suffering at all costs. The Christian outlook is not to avoid suffering but to acknowledge that we all suffer and can learn from it, so that suffering has value. It doesn't mean we seek out needless suffering, but when we encounter it, how we deal with it is what matters most. Does it become a weight that ruins lives? Or is it like the suffering a woman experiences during childbirth—pain we can use to bring tremendous beauty, value, and good into the world?

PART III

FOLLOWING MY PATH

CHAPTER 9

Learning the Trades

BY THE time Gina and I were settled into married life and raising our children, I had been making a living working with my hands for years. The steady paychecks from ironwork paid the bills and kept food on the table, but something was missing. I was trading time for dollars, building other people's dreams while my own remained undefined. What I didn't realize was that the foundation for something deeper had already been laid years earlier.

When I moved to Post Falls in 1997 after boot camp, I stumbled into Paul Settani's woodshop and discovered a whole new world—one in which working with my hands could be about so much more than just earning a paycheck. It could be about creating something that would outlast me.

Paul ran the Schola at Immaculate Conception and had welcomed me when I first joined. A short, wiry guy in his early forties with glasses, Paul had a ton of energy. He was passionate about everything he did and threw himself into his work. He also owned a woodshop and, for the past fifteen years, had made a living selling the furniture he built. As Paul and I grew close, I spent more time at his shop, helping with some of his projects. When I returned to Post Falls in 2000, Paul was still living life with the same vigor. And we picked right back up where we had left off.

Paul had just built a massive ten-foot-long dining table for a potential buyer who decided at the last minute that they didn't want it. He wasn't paid for the table and he didn't have a home for it. My folks needed a dining table. They had one, but it was way too small for everyone to sit down and eat together. I told Paul that if he gifted the table to my parents, I'd make it up to him by doing whatever was needed around the shop.

Through Paul, I learned the basics of woodworking and furniture making. He taught me how the sales side of the business worked. Then I started reading books and ordered courses on woodworking. I quickly educated myself while simultaneously building out a shop in the garage on my property.

In 2004, Paul was diagnosed with cancer. He likely got sick from the chemicals used in the workshop. Until then, he had been relatively healthy, but he soon declined rapidly. It was painful to watch. Through it all, Paul never felt sorry for himself, because he had a gift of making it seem like everything would be okay. Paul and I shared a worldview that this life is the gateway to eternal life and our suffering and death can have tremendous value in the divine economy. In his final year, he opened a health food store and ran it with his wife until he passed away in 2005 in his mid-forties, leaving behind six children.

Paul did not want his body to go to a mortuary, so it was prepared for burial at home, cleaned and dressed by a friend of the family. Under Idaho law, this can be done if the burial is within twenty-four hours of the time of death. Since my friend Mark Eberlein and I were building the casket, that didn't give us much time, but we still put care into its construction. The casket was made of oak and oak plywood, and since the chemical finishes likely caused Paul's cancer, we finished the casket with hand-applied wax. The funeral would not be open casket, so there was no need for linings or satins.

On the day of the funeral, I watched as the casket was lowered into the ground. I thought about my family and their future. *What would happen to my boys if I were to pass away? How would they remember me?* I didn't want to lose precious years spending my time away from family. My dad had traveled extensively for work when I was young, and that separation compounded many of the issues he battled with Ria. I didn't want that for my family, so I searched for a different source of steady work that would allow me to remain at home.

I was twenty-nine, and the work for which I was most qualified—and where I could earn the most money—was ironwork. That's what I always turned back to when the alternatives didn't pan out. It was reliable work, but it wasn't local. What if, instead of working for someone else, I went into business, making furniture and selling it for a profit, like Paul had? I had been honing my woodworking skills and was confident in my ability. In 2006, I decided to give it a go. I finished building out my shop in the garage, and that became the home base. Inspired by the small wooden manager that Jesus was placed in after his birth, I named the company Bethlehem Woodworks.

I understood the importance of marketing in the success of any business. In the back of *Fine Woodworking Magazine*, there was an advertisement for marketing a woodworking company. I signed up for their monthly newsletter and marketing program, which included a variety of study materials.

The program frequently mentioned the work of a marketing expert named Jay Abraham. After I had learned everything the program had to teach, I decided to go right to the source and enroll in Jay's program, an extensive, multi-hour course with exercises and study materials. The package included a one-on-one call with Jay every two weeks.

Jay's approach to conversations could be off-putting. If you did what you said you were going to do, all went well, and he would work with you on the next steps. If you didn't keep your end of the bargain, he could get a little brusque. Jay wanted all of our questions thought out and submitted in advance. If you didn't do that, he would respectfully decline to talk to you. Fortunately, I liked him immediately and the two of us quickly hit it off. He took genuine interest in what I was doing. It was the beginning of what would become a two-decade-long mentorship.

When it came to marketing, it was the little things that initially had the biggest impact. I drafted flyers advertising benches I could build and placed them on the windshields of cars parked in the church parking lot. I figured this would target families who needed more seats in their homes. And I was right! From that first batch of flyers, I sold six benches. A $5 investment in paper and photocopying yielded approximately $2,000 in business revenue. That was real leverage.

All of my work was made to order. I sold some cabinet sets. I made a nice bookcase for an elderly woman who wanted it for her living room. I came up with a design using European steamed beech that evolved into a freestanding shelf with hand-cut dovetails at the top and mortise and tenon joinery at the bottom. I did most of the work by hand, even carving lambs tongue motifs at the end of hand-planed chamfers. It was simple but beautiful. There was something special about the sound of a plane on wood, slicing a wooden ribbon so razor-thin that you could see the light through it as it peeled away. There was satisfaction in the work I was doing.

I loved the creative process and the work that went into building a piece of furniture from scratch. I have a coatrack I made during this period, and it has moved with me throughout the years. It's a functional and beautiful part of my life. I often look at it and think, *Wow! I made this eighteen years ago, and it's still holding up*. Some of the practice pieces I created then—those made to hone my skills—I still have today. A bookshelf that started as a bench but was too skinny, so I repurposed it to hold the trinkets and knickknacks in my office. The hammer veneering and hand-cut dovetails on a cabinet in my office where, even after twenty years, the mortise and tenon joints remain intact. Most furniture makers today use routers, shapers, machines, and jigs to make dovetails, but it's not the same as doing it by hand. They don't join together the same, they don't have the same strength, and they definitely don't look the same.

I take pride in looking at those pieces. It's the same feeling I get when driving through a city and seeing one of the buildings I helped erect. Every time I pass through Spokane and see the Grand Hotel, I get that feeling. It happens whenever I'm in Seattle, Portland, or any of the other places where I've worked and spot a structure that I helped to build. No one person is responsible for creating a building themselves, but there is something valuable in being part of the team that worked together to accomplish that massive project. While building furniture was a solitary pursuit that allowed me to get lost in my head, there was a different type of satisfaction when working with a team that could communicate and click. Both resulted in creating something tangible. Something concrete.

Bethlehem Woodworking was always a side hustle. I was still working in construction, but I was scaling back to spend more time at home. I became what they called a two-county boomer. A boomer is a slang term for a tradesman who travels into another jurisdiction. As a result, I became a tradesman who only worked in the nearest two counties, meaning I didn't actually travel. And because I didn't travel, I wasn't getting as much work as I used to. I was home every night, and I made an effort to get the woodworking business up and running, but in the fall of 2006, after about eight months, I realized that I wasn't making enough money. I couldn't envision a future where I would ever make enough money selling furniture. I went back to working construction to pay the bills, and it was good that I did, because there was more change on the horizon.

For a long time, Gina had wanted to move. Our trailer was situated on a fairly busy road, one that was not ideal for the kids to ride their bikes. There were no sidewalks, and some cars would whip down that winding country road at forty-five miles per hour or more. That made going for walks a dangerous proposition, especially on weekend nights when folks would speed down the road in their sports cars or motorcycles looking for a thrill. More than anything else, we wanted more land and to be out in the country. I had always wanted to live on a small-scale farm, and when I discussed it with Gina, she liked the idea as well. I wanted my kids to learn about the realities of life by growing up on a farm.

In February 2007, we found a farmhouse for sale near Worley, Idaho, about thirty miles south of Post Falls. It was located on forty acres, much of which had gone fallow, right on the Washington state line off Highway 58. There was a tiny farmhouse, a big shop, an equally big barn, and a pond on the edge of the property. It felt like a great place to raise children.

There was a lot we could do with forty acres, especially with small-scale farming methods. What particularly appealed to us was the large storage shop on the property. We could rent it out as RV storage space. There was probably room to fit thirty RVs inside, and there was a need in the area. The extra cash would help pay the mortgage so we could work the farm without worrying about house payments.

We made an offer to the owner with that in mind, but he had other plans. He had built his own house across the street but was still using the storage shop to keep generations of family junk. He insisted that he couldn't clear it out in time for us to move in. We needed to be able to rent out the storage shop to make it work financially, so we didn't buy it. However, I wasn't the only one who saw the opportunity.

Orville Moe was a small-time Spokane businessman in his seventies and a colorful character. Years earlier, he had convinced a group of investors to invest in a car racing track in Airway Heights, Washington. He got the racetrack up and running, along with several auxiliary businesses, including concessions, service bays, and supply shops. The problem was that he set up those businesses as separate entities using the seed money and pocketed the profits. The courts made him sell the racetrack to make his investors whole. He took the remaining proceeds to buy the farmhouse Gina and I had been interested in purchasing so he could start an RV storage business. The only difference was that he had the cash to make it work and didn't mind waiting for the owner to clear out the space.

We couldn't buy the property, but we did arrange to rent the farmhouse from Orville. But before we could move, we needed to sell our trailer. I didn't want to list our trailer with just any real estate agent and have them search for buyers. I wanted an agent who would work with us and who had potential buyers ready to go. I called upon my recently acquired marketing and copywriting skills to take a more creative approach. I wrote a letter explaining why we wanted to move, but I wrote it in crayon as if it were written by one of my sons. The letter shared how great it would be for the family to live on a farm, but how we first needed to find a buyer for our house. I printed ten color copies of the letter and sent it to ten prospective agents.

In June 2007, one of the agents responded. She had a potential buyer in mind, and that's whom we ended up selling the house to. It might have sold had we acquired an agent the traditional way, but we did it a little differently, and I think we made a good deal.

Using unconventional methods to attract an agent helped me see the long-term potential in the marketing skills I had acquired. The woodworking business might not have panned out, but it taught me how to use leverage to get an outsized return for my time investment. With any business, you want to reach a point where you stop trading time for dollars and start trading value for dollars. If you can get the same return for one hour of work that you can get for one hundred, why not opt for the former? I knew that I could help local businesses generate more value by using what I had learned from Jay Abraham. The plan wasn't for me to do the actual marketing but rather to evaluate the strategy and identify potential clients that local businesses were overlooking.

Gina and I set aside a significant portion of the money from the sale of the home to pay for our next house. We then invested another portion in a series of CDs from the local bank. We arranged it so that each month, one of the CDs would mature, and we'd receive a new influx of cash to pay that month's bills. The rest of the money I put into the new marketing business, Northwest Venture Marketing. It was a nice chunk of change to get started, but I was still working on a budget. I promised to call it quits if I was unable to get traction before I ran out of cash. That was my stop-loss point, and it was nonnegotiable. If it didn't happen, I'd fold the business and move on.

I turned one corner of the boys' bedroom into an office and set up shop—with four sons and another on the way, it was already a tight squeeze. I signed three local clients right away—a print shop, a financial planning company, and a dentist. They trusted me, and I was able to stir up some extra business for each of them.

Business was good. I generated traction early, but revenue soon plateaued. It didn't help that my office (i.e., the farmhouse) was thirty miles outside Post Falls. Any given day, I easily put one hundred miles on the car, driving out to Post Falls and Coeur d'Alene to do business in town. That proved inconvenient and ate up a great deal of time and money, not to mention wear and tear on the car. After six months, I was unable to attract enough new clients to consistently turn a profit.

By late fall of 2007, I realized I couldn't make the numbers work. I sat down on the floor of my office, leaned against the bedroom wall, and cried. It wasn't just the money—it was what this failure said about me. Here I was, thirty-one years old, and I couldn't make a single business idea stick. First the woodworking; now the marketing venture. Both were dead in the water. Maybe everyone back on the jobsite who thought I was crazy for trying to go into business for myself was right.

I kept thinking about the conversation I'd have to have with Gina. She'd been so supportive when I wanted to try something different and never once made me feel guilty about the irregular income or the risks we took. How was I supposed to look her in the eye and tell her I had failed again? The kids were too young to understand, but it felt like I had let them down, too.

The worst part was facing my clients. I'd promised them more clients and higher revenue. These people had trusted me with their livelihoods; they believed I could help them grow their businesses when I couldn't even keep my own afloat. I would have to call each one and admit that I was folding the business—the guy who was supposed to have all the answers didn't know what he was doing.

When I finally picked up the phone to make those calls my hands were shaking, but I sucked it up and I had those difficult conversations. It turned out that all my fears were in my head. Not one client had the negative reaction I had expected. They understood, thanked me for my efforts, and wished me well. Gina wasn't disappointed either. She knew that I was going back to work and welcomed having a regular paycheck and health insurance again. I put my tool belt back on and returned to ironwork. Nobody made me feel like a failure and I was welcomed back into the fold.

The two businesses I had started didn't pan out, but that wouldn't be the end of my entrepreneurial efforts. Ironically, I would soon make my mark in the one industry I had been desperately trying to leave.

My father had made a name for himself by increasing the profitability of the installation side of the precast construction business for companies. He was the best at what he did, and he worked on some major projects throughout his career, such as orchestrating the erection process of the giant roof trusses in the Delta Center where the Utah Jazz play. He had experience running jobs, making money, and dealing with problems. Through his leadership ethos and skill as a tradesman, his team was able to perform at a higher level, which resulted in a bigger return. Some of the companies he worked for had been unable to turn a profit from their installation work before he began running jobs. That made him a valuable commodity, and it created a unique opportunity for us.

Now, let's say you're building a parking garage, office building, or any other concrete structure. You can have cement trucks on-site and pour concrete into forms laid out for one section, wait for the concrete to turn hard and gray, and then move to the next section. That's a good process, but it's time-consuming, labor-intensive, and potentially expensive. Another option is to have precast concrete made in a factory setting with factory labor. It's exactly what it sounds like: concrete pieces cast before they get to the site. The pieces can be quite large and can be made at the same time the site is being prepped. Those larger pieces are then assembled on-site. The process requires significantly fewer on-site workers and has less impact on the surrounding neighborhood. It's also much faster. That's where precast fits into the construction market. It's a more cost-effective and efficient alternative. Most companies that sell and install precast concrete make their money on the sale of the precast concrete. The installation is simply an add-on service, priced at a discount, allowing the company to sell more precast products.

While my dad worked for multiple companies, he received the most work from Central Premix. They assigned him to work with different developers on individual projects; one of those developers was Walt Worthy. All of their projects together went well. In 2005, when Walt planned to build a hotel tower in downtown Spokane, he asked my father to oversee the project. At the last minute, Central Premix pulled him off Walt's job and shipped him to Madras, Oregon, instead to oversee the construction of a prison for a different developer. It was a more difficult job, and Central Premix wanted someone running it who wouldn't require handholding.

My father took me to Oregon as his road partner and right-hand man on the project, which went quite well. We were so far ahead of schedule that, on most days, we finished our work by 11 a.m. and spent the rest of the day fishing together at a local lake. Meanwhile, Central Premix had put a different superintendent on Walt's hotel tower project, and that didn't go nearly as well. Walt felt betrayed by Central Premix, so in 2007, before beginning construction on his new office building in Spokane, he took control of the process and independently reached out to my father to run it.

This was an opportunity for my dad and me to go into business. There was a risk, but it was one worth taking, because there was clearly a need for this type of work. However, my dad worried that if he worked directly for Walt, he would never be hired by Central Premix again. Why do that? He was already in a leadership role. He had a company truck and people working underneath him. At fifty-five, his days as a worker bee were numbered, so maintaining a leadership role was a good way to comfortably extend his career until he reached retirement.

After a few months of mulling the decision over, eventually my father came around. We decided to take on Walt's office building and start our own business. But if we were going to take this step, it needed to be worthwhile. I saw an opportunity to negotiate the fee structure.

Walt was covering the cost; Central Premix was providing the materials. Walt wanted to pay us a flat fee of $50,000 to plan and lead the installation. Instead, I devised an incentive-based agreement that would pay us more if we brought the project in ahead of schedule. The idea was to under-promise and over-deliver, but Walt thought our first target was too low, so it required further negotiation. We settled on a four-month time frame and incentives that could pay us up to $185,000 for a project for which they originally intended to pay $50,000. Of course, if there were delays, we would receive a lower payment. If we dropped the ball entirely, we could end up with nothing. It was a huge risk, but the upside was worth it.

We finalized negotiations in December 2007 and began work

on the project in April 2008. Walt signed a one-year agreement with the union, which allowed us to hire union workers. And since the project was right in Spokane, and everyone wanted to work near home, we had no difficulty finding guys.

While covering the day-to-day cash flow wouldn't be our responsibility on this job, any delays in the delivery of materials from the manufacturer could prevent us from hitting our targets. To avoid shipping issues, we selected the trucking company for the deliveries—Robinet Trucking. We provided an added incentive for them to meet our delivery schedule (and show off their capabilities in the process). Robinet ultimately performed at a very high level. Central Premix (who was still providing the materials) also sought to regain Walt Worthy's trust, so they made sure they were not the problem on the project. It was good business for them to repair the relationship.

I knew we were capable of finishing ahead of schedule, but the project went even better than I had thought it would. We completed the four-month job twenty-five days ahead of schedule and earned the full potential incentive of $185,000. My dad and I were now officially in business together! That was the start of Precision Precast Erectors (PPE).

Construction is a unique industry with a diverse range of companies and contractors of varying interests, needs, and commitments, all working on a multitude of different projects. The people running each project believe that they are important and that the contractor should prioritize their success. The reality is that contractors are often spread thin. They might tell you they're going to arrive at a particular time, only to be pulled off the job because another client on another project was yelling louder, so they went to fix that problem. As a result, construction companies, and contractors in particular, are not known for being professional, timely, or committed to schedules.

My dad and I didn't have a big company with deep pockets behind us. We had a limited amount of cash, which proved to be a significant challenge that put us at a disadvantage. To set ourselves apart, we pitched ourselves as the only independent experts who were highly schedule-driven and professional. We would represent the client like no other and make their precast look amazing.

My dad and I drew up an operating agreement with us as equal partners. We did the estimating together, but because I had small business experience, I did more of the sales and legwork—visiting jobsites and shaking hands with contractors. He ran the jobsites.

We knew this wouldn't be a huge moneymaker at first and that if we paid ourselves in between jobs, we would use up all our money. During those first few years, we conserved our capital and worked as employees of other ironworking companies to pay the bills until we landed a new contract for PPE. That gave us the flexibility to take time off to run the business.

My furniture business wasn't a success, but it had taught me how hard it is to do everything yourself. I was trying to build the furniture, sell the product, finance the business, and do the marketing—there weren't enough hours in the day, and the business suffered as a result. I wouldn't make that same mistake again.

When getting PPE off the ground, I could immediately tell that I didn't have a knack for keeping the books. My first attempt at handling payroll, while keeping track of all the expenses for a small job, was a nightmare. I was more than willing to pay someone else to perform the tasks I was not good at, so I hired a small bookkeeping company (Clear Management, owned by Amelia McCalmont) to do everything from payroll to data entry. That minor detail might have been the single most important factor in our success.

Many small businesses and start-ups attempt to handle their own bookkeeping, but because they lack expertise, they can encounter issues with the IRS and the unions. Neither of those entities plays nicely, so mistakes can be expensive. The money we paid the bookkeeping company to keep us above water and prevent any avoidable legal fees was worth it. Hiring people individually to serve these functions in-house would have cost three times as much.

After our first job with Walt, we landed some smaller jobs that kept us afloat. In 2009, we bid for the job that would eventually give us our big break—the South Correctional Entity, a prison in Des Moines, Washington, about sixteen miles south of Seattle.

Until that point, our largest project had generated a $180,000 revenue. The contract price for this job was $765,000. At four months' duration, it was also longer than the previous jobs we had been offered. We were awarded the bid, but unlike our first job with Walt Worthy, our expenses on this one would be much higher—we couldn't cover them on our own. Cash flow would be a problem. After crunching the numbers, I realized we needed an extra $100,000 to cover our costs.

Every bank I talked to said the same thing: "We don't lend money to people in construction." This was just after the 2008–2009 housing crisis, and the industry as a whole was deemed too risky. Finally, I found a bank that would give us a $100,000 line of credit. But there was a catch: We needed to deposit $100,000 into the bank.

We didn't have $100,000, so I found two private hard-money lenders—private investors or companies that provide short-term loans at higher interest rates with a faster approval process. I borrowed $50,000 from one at 6 percent interest and $50,000 from the other at 12 percent interest. That gave me the $100,000 to deposit into the bank so that I could secure a line of credit and borrow from the bank at 6 percent. We were basically paying 18 percent interest, but it was the only way to get the cash flow needed to complete the job. That was difficult to swallow, but there was no choice. The situation was simple: If the job didn't go well, we would be out of business. That put a whole new level of pressure on us to perform.

With no margin for error, I learned how to make detailed cash flow projections and break down cost structures. I knew exactly when cash would come in and when it would go out. There was no wiggle room, so we couldn't afford to be wrong. But that wasn't the only lesson I learned on that job.

Hans was the project manager who worked for the general

contractor overseeing the project. At six foot one and 350 pounds, he was an imposing figure, and he knew what he was doing. Hans wasn't ashamed to take advantage of an inexperienced contractor like myself. When I negotiated with him, he got me to put up the money for the payment bond (which guarantees subcontractors, suppliers, and laborers will be paid for their work and materials if we were to default), something that normally shouldn't be our responsibility. That mistake cost PPE $20,000.

There were times when Hans and my father got into shouting matches over change orders. I don't know what my dad said to him, but he got Hans to come around more often than not. At other times, they staged their arguments to prepare other subcontractors and suppliers for a problem on the horizon, making it appear as though my dad was fighting on their behalf. Another savvy move.

Fortunately, we caught a few breaks on this job. There were some delays where we'd work for two or three weeks and then take a week or two off. Normally, that would be a problem, but since the loan was for one year, the delays allowed more time to balance the books so that we didn't fall too far into debt. Thankfully, the job went well and, when it completed in July 2009, we were able to pay back our investors and lenders. That was a learning experience, and it marked a turning point for PPE, enabling the business to take off.

CHAPTER 10

Working with Family, Building a Family

THE MASSIVE chain-link fence surrounding our home should have been my first clue. Every morning when I left for work, I had to stop the truck, get out, unlock the gate, drive through, then get out to lock the gate behind me.

We had been living at the farmhouse for a year when, in 2010, the previous owner finally cleaned out the storage shed and Orville set up his RV storage business. He had built a large chain-link fence around the entire property that made it feel like living in a compound. Orville's family members were always there working at the storage barn, and his wife would come knocking on our front door the second of every month looking for the rent. While the farmhouse had a lot of land, it never really felt like the house was ours. Plus, we were running out of room. Gina's Aunt Reggie had come to live with us, and by the end of the year, Gina was pregnant again, so we began searching for a new home

Gina came across an ad for a property she liked and drove out with the kids to take a look. About a half hour outside Post Falls, the house was located on a private road and set on ten acres of wilderness, making it an ideal remote location. She wanted me to look at it and gave me directions so I could drive out there and see it for myself.

Following her directions, I turned onto a dirt road. As I approached the forest, I saw a massive, rusty steel sign that looked like something out of an apocalyptic wasteland. Hand-painted in big letters, it read: "Warning! Keep Out! No Boat Access! Violators Will Be Prosecuted!" What it was really saying was: "Violators will be shot dead on sight and then prosecuted for trespassing and spoiling the ground with their blood and guts."

I took one look at that sign and assumed I had to be on the wrong road, so I turned around. When I saw Gina back at home, I told her about the sign. "Oh, no. That's the right road," she said. "Don't worry about it. Just keep going." The sign that had intimidated me, she had no problem ignoring. Gina had grown up in the woods; she knew that signs were there to discourage hunters, motorcyclists, and UTVs that often leave a torn-up mess in their wake.

The next day, I went back and drove past the sign, down a long, winding road through the forest. There were about twenty other houses all spread out and with a lot of land in between, but only one way in or out before the road came to a dead end a few miles past the sign.

I found the house, and calling it a work in progress would be charitable. The bank had repossessed the house in 2008 at the start of the housing crash. It was 2,800 square feet, so it had been put on the market for the absurdly high price of $325,000—without realizing that the previous owner had gutted the inside. The house lacked heat and a functional kitchen, with rooms of odd shapes and sizes. Technically, it was listed as a one-bedroom, two-bath, but the bedroom was massive—almost eighteen by thirty-six feet—and there was no closet or storage space.

When no one showed interest in buying the house, the bank

lowered the price by roughly $10,000 every month. This price continued to drop for fourteen months until it fell below $200,000. Meanwhile, the house deteriorated.

We knew that renovating this house would be a project, but we also saw the potential. After negotiating the price down to $165,000, we signed in April 2009. The market was at rock bottom, so despite the house's poor condition, it was a savvy buy. Of course, it also wasn't livable. We had to remain at the farmhouse for a few more months while we applied for a construction loan to begin renovations.

The job at the correctional facility in Des Moines, Washington, had finished in May 2009, which proved to be good timing. A few months later in July, Gina gave birth to our fifth son, Francis (named after Saint Francis of Assisi, whom I view as a pinnacle of the Evangelical Counsels), inside the farmhouse. The midwives arrived in time to assist, and all went well.

While Gina cared for the boys at home, I worked on making our new house livable. I installed the kitchen floor, cabinets, and appliances and hired a contractor to help with the interior renovation. We converted the huge bedroom into two, which allowed us to have an extra bedroom for the boys. The contractor built closets in the new room so that it could legally be called a bedroom. The electrical needed to be rewired, and both the interior and exterior needed to be repainted. Since the house still had no heat, I installed a woodstove and a radiant ceiling panel heating system, which is more efficient than floorboard radiators and doesn't occupy any floor space. We added a storage pantry and a huge farmhouse-style dining table in the middle of the kitchen, one that was big enough for me, Gina, and our five boys to all comfortably fit.

I loved the house because it was the antithesis of suburbia. The property had a savage wilderness quality to it. We let the grass grow tall so that the seed heads waved in the wind. We listened to wild turkeys gobble in the distance and chased away the occasional moose who ventured onto the property. Of course, nothing remained calm for long.

By 2011, it seemed like life had found its groove: PPE was growing, the wilderness house was becoming home, and Gina was pregnant with our sixth son. We'd soon learn that this birth would test everything we believed about bringing children into the world on our own terms.

Once again, we were planning for a home birth, but as the November due date neared, the midwives worried that Gina was trending toward preeclampsia again, though not nearly as bad as with the twins. That meant that we would have to give birth in a hospital.

It's normal when working with a midwife to also have a relationship with a doctor in case the mother needs medical intervention during or after the delivery. The challenge for us was that insurance companies considered vaginal birth after C-section (VBAC) to be "high risk." Despite three successful VBAC deliveries, our previous doctor wouldn't consent to be our backup option, nor would any doctor in the Coeur d'Alene area. The nearest hospital with a doctor who would agree to serve as our backup was at Sacred Heart Medical Center, a one-hour drive away in Spokane. We'd been there a few times for prenatal checkups, but with their hospitalist program, you are assigned whatever doctor happens to be on shift at the time of your appointment. Gina never saw the same doctor twice, so there was no established relationship with an obstetrician.

On the morning of November 6, 2011, Gina went into labor. We piled into our red and silver 1997 Suburban, dropped the boys off at Gina's brother Pat's house, and made the hour-long drive to Sacred Heart. Gina remained calm the whole way, spending most of the ride staring out the window and focused on her breathing. I was nervous, anxious to get there, but I didn't want her to see that, so I kept quiet, held her hand, and concentrated on the road ahead. We drove most of the way in silence.

Upon arriving at the hospital, I pulled up to the valet and rushed around to the passenger side to help ease Gina out of the car. We made our way inside, checked in, and the hospital staff quickly cleared a room for us. That sterile, hospital environment was uncomfortable, and from there, the situation only worsened. Gina was exposed, poked, and prodded by a dozen nurses and staff members who were coming and in and out of our hospital room. It was intolerable, and it deeply violated her sense of modesty and safety.

When the female obstetrician arrived, she was curt and contemptuous. It was the first time she had laid eyes on us, yet she tried to make us feel as if we were stupid for having a sixth child and even stupider for not having an established and regular OBGYN. This was surprising because she was a woman yet was much less understanding and compassionate than some of the male doctors we'd had in the past. That made for a very unpleasant experience for both of us.

There was one kind nurse—she had a history of working with midwives and had assisted in many natural births. She respected women like Gina who chose a more natural path and promised to be respectful of our wishes. And while that was comforting, it didn't relieve the palpable tension.

For a brief moment, the doctors and hospital staff left us alone in the room. Gina grabbed my hand and asked me to help her to the bathroom. I should have known something was up. In the eight years we had been married, she had never asked me to help her to the bathroom. Once we were inside, she told me to lock the bathroom door. Then she sat down on the bathroom floor and prepared to deliver our child.

I panicked. While I may have been in this situation before, I didn't feel any more comfortable delivering my child, but this wasn't about me. After the way we had been treated, I respected Gina's decision. We had done it before, and I knew we could do it again, so I settled down. We stayed in the bathroom as the labor progressed and the contractions grew closer together. The staff knew something was up. I heard the nurses knocking on the door, asking if we needed help. "We're fine," I assured them, but I don't think they believed me.

After a few minutes, the kind nurse who respected Gina came to the door. "I understand your concern," she said. "If you unlock the door, I will work with you and only do what you're comfortable with."

"Just you?" I asked.

"Just me. I promise."

We opened the door, and the nurse quickly and calmly took control of the situation. I could finally exhale and step back. Over the next hour, the nurse calmed Gina and delivered our son, Sean, right there on the bathroom floor of the Sacred Heart Medical Center. Afterward, the nurse cut the umbilical cord and placed our baby on Gina's chest.

I forgot everything that happened outside the room and felt only relief that our baby was healthy. But the commotion on the other side of the door snapped me back to reality. The obstetrician and the rest of the hospital staff were clearly unhappy.

We didn't remain in the bathroom long. The nurse held our baby while I carefully lifted Gina to her feet. Together, the four of us returned to the delivery room, and I helped Gina lay down in bed for postpartum treatment.

The obstetrician was a bit forceful during her examination and while putting in her stitches. It felt like the rest of the staff ignored Gina, providing only the most basic medical care. During our entire stay, it felt like our wishes or desires were never factored in. Every decision was made to accommodate the doctors and the hospital, not what was best for the patient. That wasn't just sad and frustrating; it was wrong—and there has to be a better way.

Sean was our sixth son—the name a tribute to Gina's Irish heritage—and we didn't think that he would be our last child. I was thirty-five, and Gina was thirty-three. We had agreed to welcome as many children as God would give us. That's not how most people look at parenthood, but who am I to question what God wanted from us? Gina's brother and his wife struggled to have children early on, so everyone thought they would only have a few kids, but they ended up with thirteen. You never know. I believed that our family would continue to grow. In my mind, I always pictured having ten children, so that's what I'd mentally prepared for. They say that if you want to make God laugh, tell Him your plans. It's been nine years, and we haven't had any more children.

As we were establishing our family in our new home, the pressures of running a business were mounting. The success that should have brought my father and me closer together was instead driving us apart.

I tend to give people the benefit of the doubt and to look at life through rose-colored glasses. I had done this with my father most of my life. But in 2013, six years into our business partnership as we celebrated reaching $3 million in annual sales, our working relationship was tested.

We had been successful enough to take a salary and to even hire a few full-time employees. Bill Mayer was a close family friend (his son would later marry one of my sisters). For the past year, he had occasionally come in to help us work on a bid so that we could secure a job. We had been doing well enough to purchase a couple of company trucks, but we didn't have a shop yet; we were still renting.

My father and I had been making the four-and-a-half-hour drive every week to Boardman, Oregon, where we had a contract to build a potato processing plant. We spent the week at the jobsite and then returned home on weekends to be with family. It was a nine-month project and we had settled in for the long haul. I was doing the estimating, bidding, data entry, and job planning. My dad was running the crew and dealing with day-to-day issues but was clearly unhappy with the arrangement. Perhaps he regretted the 50/50 split we had agreed upon when starting the business.

One day, toward the start of the project, Bill and I were in the small office trailer on the jobsite. Bill just happened to be sitting in the same chair my father normally sat in. When Dad walked in, he took one look at Bill and said, "Get out of my f*****g chair!"

That rubbed me the wrong way. I stepped in to say, "Don't talk to him like that!"

Turns out that *I* was the person he was actually mad at. He had been holding it inside for a long time, and now he wanted a fight.

He snapped at me. "I'm so tired of your bullshit. You think you're so high and mighty, but you're hiding in the air-conditioned trailer while I'm out there busting my ass. Let's go!"

He stomped outside, I followed him, and we squared up. The whole time, he was yelling and screaming. People poked their heads out of the nearby trailers, trying to get a look at the spectacle.

My blood boiled. I had never scrapped with my dad before. I wasn't going throw the first punch, but if he swung at me, all bets were off. I was not backing down.

A few words were exchanged, and judging by the look in his eye, I could tell that he really wanted to hit me. His fists were clenched, and he was breathing heavy. He stepped forward, as if to lunge at me, then something in his expression shifted—maybe he saw the crew was watching, or remembered we were father and son—and his hands slowly released. Without another word, he turned and walked in the opposite direction, leaving me standing there, still shaking.

I went for a walk to calm down but only got more riled up. My dad was the veteran; he thought he should be the one with the cushy job, but he couldn't do what I did. He couldn't manage complex Excel workbooks and the tracking necessary to keep things flowing. He lacked experience with contracts, finances, and the legal aspects of the business. I couldn't lead crews the way he did, and he couldn't lead the company the way I did.

Our fight was nothing new. In the construction industry, office personnel are often at odds with those in the field. The field people don't think the office people work hard or know what they're doing; the office people don't think the field people respect their contribution because, without them, they wouldn't have a job. Round and round it went.

During my walk, I kept thinking of all of the trouble my dad had created in my life. He made everything difficult for those around him, and this business was no different. The signs had been there for everyone else to see, but I had chosen to ignore them. It felt like that would never change. Then I thought: *I'm done. I don't need this.*

I packed up my car and made the four-hour drive back home. On that long drive, I did a lot of thinking. By the time I pulled into my driveway, I had made up my mind. I didn't even unpack the car. Instead, I wrote a letter of resignation, drove over to his house, and dropped it in his mailbox for him to read when he returned that weekend.

Sure enough, when Saturday rolled around, I got a phone call from him. This time, he wasn't confrontational. He apologized; he wanted to keep working together. I had since calmed down, too, and I wasn't ready to walk away from everything we had built together. Sunday night, I drove back to Oregon and returned to work.

That confrontation with my father should have been a warning sign. I had thought we'd resolved our differences, but the resentment that surfaced that day was just the beginning. It would take five more years for me to fully understand how deep those fractures ran—not just in our business partnership, but in our entire family.

The relationship with my dad, while contentious, was not nearly as contentious as his relationship with Ria. By 2018, they were constantly at each other's throats. It had gotten so bad during a Christmas party the previous year that I made a speech about the importance of family and persevering through problems. Ria had reached a point where she was unable to forgive my father for the way he treated her. That made him angry and resentful. He would say, "If I'm so bad to live with, why don't you just file for divorce?" So, eventually, she did.

Ria was now in a different situation. All but one of their kids was over eighteen and out of the house, so she didn't have to rely on my dad's financial support like she used to. I tried to help them through their issues, but there were too many wounds and they were too resentful of each other to make it work.

Their divorce was painful, and what made the situation worse was that I had to explain it to our kids. Gina and I had shielded the boys from much of the dysfunction between my dad and Ria. We wanted the kids to grow up with a healthier understanding of marriage, relationships, and family, so they never witnessed the fighting or saw the true nature of their grandparents' troubled marriage. For them, the decision to divorce was a shock.

When you belong to a faith that considers marriage sacrosanct, how do you reconcile that faith with a divorce in the family? These were adults the kids were supposed to look up to; if their role models didn't stay the course, it might make the kids think that marriage wasn't that important after all.

Gina and I tried to explain to the kids the difference between how the government viewed marriage and how the Church viewed marriage. According to our faith, marriage transcends civil law—the state can grant legal divorce, but the spiritual bond remains. That meant their grandparents were separated but still married in God's eyes, and remarriage wasn't an option.

Ria received a fair amount of money from the divorce settlement and she used it to help out the rest of their kids. She worked at Walmart for a short time, then moved into the house next door which she had inherited from her parents (Mitze passed away in 2017 and Grandpa Des in 2015). In 2019, she sold that house and moved with my sister Angela and her husband down to Sanford, Florida.

While the divorce caused lots of division and sibling rivalry within the family, my dad prioritized maintaining ownership of our company and was able to negotiate the division of assets. That meant giving up his interest in the house and a substantial portion of his retirement account. He bought a house in Spokane Valley, where he lived for a year before selling it and moving back to Post Falls.

After the divorce, my dad's substance abuse issues resurfaced, and in 2019, he entered a twelve-step recovery program. The root of recovery work is acknowledging that you have problems and flaws that you need a savior to help overcome. You have to be willing to accept that we are all flawed humans. We all sin and hurt people, and we must be willing to make amends. We must change our beliefs and develop an intimate relationship with a higher power (God) to become better people so we aren't dependent on a substance or behavior to cope and feel better.

My dad had been out of control for a long time, and he was aware of it. He knew that he needed to mend his relationship with God to become a better person. Step nine is making amends, and he eventually came to me to do just that.

I was running a job in Henderson, Nevada, renting a house nearby to stay in during the week. On days when the field team had everything under control, I worked from the house. One day, my dad drove down to check on the jobsite. Afterward, he called me and asked if he could come by the house to talk privately. I assumed that it was work-related, but when he arrived and sat down across from me at the kitchen table, he caught me off guard.

"I've been working through the twelve steps," he said. "I want to make amends. I want to apologize for bringing bad things into your life."

There was a long pause. I thought he was just getting started, but he was done. To fill the silence, he said, "Can you forgive me?"

That was his apology. It was that generic.

I'll give him credit for making the effort, and at the time, I forgave him. I came away from the interaction underwhelmed by what felt like a generic apology, one that failed to acknowledge all the rotten things he did to me, my siblings, my mother, and Ria. His behavior had an impact on me growing up, and it would continue to have an impact on me as an adult, but that's not what I heard. What I heard was, "I feel guilty, and I'll feel less guilty if you forgive me." I knew that, given his personality, trying to force him to truly make amends would be unproductive. Once again, I didn't get from him what I needed at the time—but he couldn't give me something that he didn't have.

To his credit, my dad is still clean and sober today. It has had a positive impact on his life and our family dynamic, but it didn't make him easier to work with. He would later contribute to what would soon become the biggest test of my life.

CHAPTER 11

The Darkest Hour

BY 2021, the cracks were showing—in my marriage, in my business partnership with my father, and in my ability to hold everything together. I just didn't know that all those fractures were about to converge into the darkest moment of my life.

My dad's dreams of early retirement went out the window after the divorce. After having a blockage removed from his carotid artery in 2019, he thought about his mortality and started reconsidering retirement. I conducted extensive research and legwork, exploring conventional commercial lending avenues that would provide me with the necessary funds to buy him out. The loan would cover the operating expenses of the business, allowing me to use receivables to buy his shares from him. Still, I was unable to find a suitable package that met our needs.

During the fall of 2021, at the tail end of the COVID-19 pandemic, we learned about a COVID-19-related loan program where businesses could borrow up to $2 million from the Small Business Administration to cover operating expenses on a thirty-year term. This loan was a way for us to make the numbers work. The only catch was that we had to file by December 31, 2021, and it was already October. Applying didn't guarantee we would get the loan—our application still had to be reviewed and approved. But in order to apply, my dad and I first had to agree on the terms of the buyout.

The business was appraised at $3–3.5 million, and considering the excess working capital in the business, the total value was between $4.5 and $5 million. Together with my legal counsel, we crafted what I felt was a fair offer—25 percent above the market price. It's important to note business sales done internally tend to be below market value, while deals done with outside investors, particularly strategic investors, can be at or above market value.

My father would be paid a token amount, roughly $1,000 a month, along with his regular salary, until the money arrived. We'd then use the loan to pay operating expenses, since that was the purpose of the loan. As the receivables came in, that money would be used to pay my dad off over roughly six months. There was always the possibility that the loan wouldn't be approved, in which case we would unwind the deal, no harm, no foul. The upside was that he would walk away with a little over $2.5 million in cash. Done. Easy. That's a very good deal for a small business buyout because if you're paid over a longer period and the business fails, you could be left with nothing. The deal was a win for someone trying to retire and get out of the business.

In the weeks leading up to the end-of-year filing deadline, we batted a few offers back and forth. We had a lot of potential future work on the books, and my dad didn't want to miss out on those profits. He would get hung up on some minor details in the contract, such as the interest rate. He also wanted significantly more money up front and insisted on retaining it, regardless of whether the deal went through, which seemed unreasonable. He wanted to have his cake and eat it, too. At that last minute, we reached an impasse. He was never happy with the terms, but I believe there was something else going on beneath the surface.

Everything is a competition with my dad. He hates losing, so he tries to one-up everyone whenever possible, especially me. A few weeks before the COVID-19 lockdowns in 2020, he came with me to a Harley dealership to help me shop for my first motorcycle. I showed him the blue and purple two-tone bike I had been eyeing. It often takes me a long time to make a decision. While I was mulling it over, he went out a few days later and bought the same bike. Maybe he didn't think I would follow through, but he still couldn't wait to show it off. Now I couldn't buy it anymore, so I bought a different motorcycle.

In the business, our salaries always had to be equal. Since our situations were very different, my dad paid more taxes. That led to resentment and frustration. He felt like he was always getting screwed because so much of his money went to paying taxes—and I always walked away with a bigger chunk of cash.

When it came to the buyout, he felt he was getting left behind—that he was getting cut out of the upcoming financial windfall that he was responsible for. This was compounded by years of resentment that left him feeling like he was the one who had started the company and had done all the work. Worse, he thought that I was trying to take advantage of him. Pulling out of the deal, he said, "I don't trust that you're going to pay me. I don't think you can do this. I'm out. I'm not selling."

That gut punch felt like my world had shattered. Our relationship had been more strained than ever since his divorce from Ria, and this was the culmination of much stress and confrontation that had built up over the previous years. I had put so much energy into making this deal happen. What hurt most was that he was my dad, and he didn't trust me. He didn't believe that I would do the right thing. Instead, he thought I was trying to take advantage of him, to take a bigger piece of the company when I meant to do the complete opposite. I offered 25 percent above market value—an offer that put *me* at a disadvantage. If he said no to that offer, under what conditions would he ever say yes? It felt like he didn't even know me, and that devastated me.

The deal fell apart on the morning of our annual company Christmas party. Those parties are intense and emotionally draining because I put a lot of effort into appreciating all the employees who have helped make the business such a success. Now, I had to put on a happy face and sit next to my dad, who didn't trust me and thought I was out to get him.

The party, while difficult, proved to be a nice distraction for a few hours. I always enjoyed seeing everyone we worked with in one location. But after that brief respite ended, I was reminded of my father as soon as Gina and I got in the truck to drive home. It didn't help that we had been struggling, too. As we drove, I said, "I would just like to hold your hand."

"No, not tonight," she said.

We got home, and I went to bed alone, so exhausted and drained that I fell asleep immediately. I woke up the next morning with an overwhelming sense of hopelessness and despair. It always takes some time for emotions to work their way through my body—it must have been a symptom of my delayed emotional processing—but I wasn't prepared for this intensity. Lying there in bed, I felt my world closing in on me. I was suffocating, uncomfortable in my own skin, and the only way I could escape was to harm myself—to end my own life.

That was a completely foreign feeling, one much different than my experience with the evil presence in the monastery. This felt like I was outside my body, watching another part of me take charge. Never had I contemplated suicide before—I had never even considered it a possibility—but it felt like I had no control. I didn't want to hurt myself, yet I had the urge to die and was powerless to intervene.

The problem was there were two guns next to me. One on the left under the bedside table and one on the right under Gina's pillow. If I moved, or made any attempt to get out of bed, it would bring me one step closer to those guns, to committing suicide. I didn't trust myself.

But there weren't any guns in the walk-in closet in the corner of the room. That was the safest place that I could go—my only refuge. I just had to make it across the room. I crawled on the floor toward the closet, got inside, and shut the door behind me, so it was pitch-black. I curled up in the fetal position on the floor, wrapped tight in a blanket. It felt like being in a womb. There I stayed, waiting for the moment to pass. I don't know if it was a minute later or an hour when finally Gina entered the bedroom. The closet door is always open, so it's obvious that's where I was. She knocked on the door and asked if I was okay.

"I'm not okay," I said.

"Is there anything I can do?" she asked.

There wasn't, but the fact that she tried to come in and talk helped. Still, I wasn't coming out any time soon. I had to ride this out. I had to remind myself that my emotions were not evil; they were not trying to harm me. They were just part of the human system—a feature, not a bug. The only harm would come from trying to repress them or to pretend they didn't exist.

Some people consider negative emotions a weakness or a character flaw. What they fail to understand is that our emotions serve an important function, even unpleasant emotions like sadness, frustration, and envy.

I believe our body and souls are connected systems; the body is the vessel in which those emotions are contained. Emotions can produce different physical sensations, like the way your heart skips around a new love, or the fire of a heated argument. Those sensations compel us to act on those emotions, for better or worse. And when experiencing an unpleasant emotion, that action is almost always worse. But by acknowledging those emotions—focusing on the sensations attached to them and allowing them to run their course—you can emerge on the other side having learned something valuable. You need to experience it, acknowledge it, and even appreciate it as proof that you are fully human. That's what I was trying to do.

After about three hours, the urge to harm myself had worked its way through my body. As Galadriel says, "I passed the test." I felt it was safe to leave the closet. I didn't know what to do with myself, so I carried on as though nothing had happened. I didn't tell anyone about my experience, and that left me alone to wrestle with what had occurred.

The Church condemns suicide as a grave sin. Suicide is commonly referred to as the "coward's way out" and we are told we're going to hell if we take our own life. I've never fully agreed with that stance, understanding instead that those who commit suicide are often not in their right mind. And if they are not in their right mind, then they can't be held accountable for their actions. Suicide is not a philosophical or theoretical problem; it's a deep emotional, neurological, and psychological problem. The belief is that the will is supreme and we can conquer anything, but will alone cannot conquer true mental illness. I don't know how a God of pure love could condemn someone who is clearly consumed by a mental illness. That should not prevent anyone from experiencing the love of God.

My experience didn't change my beliefs; it increased my level of compassion for those who struggle with suicidal thoughts. A friend of mine refers to this as one of "the diseases of despair" and I've seen how these diseases are woven throughout aspects of our society. It starts with what we do and how we define ourselves. It's easy to believe that the value we bring to the world can be directly traced back to what we do for a paycheck, so if we're not generating income, that can be demoralizing. Couple that with the various traumas and heartache we all experience, and that leads to a lot of pain and suffering. Many people suffer in silence, and we don't realize how much they're suffering until it's too late. There's a saying in business that "what gets measured, matters," but it applies to life as well. We need to celebrate a person's life in different ways. After all, no one puts their salary on a tombstone.

It's taken a very long time and a lot of personal work to get to a place where I feel comfortable speaking openly about what I experienced in that closet. I've tried to use my experience to help others better understand the root cause of these diseases of despair. I've spoken with friends at church who have struggled with these issues themselves, or who've had children who struggled.

When one of my good friends opened up to me about how he was frustrated was with a former colleague and friend of ours who took his own life after losing a battle with addiction, I was able to share my experience and let him know that our colleague probably didn't want to do what he did. It might have happened despite what he wanted. I shared how I felt when I experienced the urge to harm myself and how it's not always a conscious decision. More often than not, it's a spontaneous thought that can almost take possession and overwhelm us despite our intentions.

I like to believe that by sharing my experience I can help others or at least help them better understand the mental state of someone who feels compelled to harm themselves. It's not easy to comprehend; it's a process that took me a long time and a lot of work to understand myself.

The morning I locked myself in that closet was one of the strangest, and most significant, days of my life because it's what inspired me to change. Afterward, I reflected on what had happened and tried to figure out what I needed to do next. I was going to Mass daily, trying to wrap my head around my relationship with my father and what I was supposed to do about the business. I didn't have any answers. I just knew that I needed to work on myself in earnest and figure out whose approval I was really seeking.

CHAPTER 12

Chipping Away at the Rough Edges

FOR MOST of my adult life, long before that day in the closet, I knew I needed help, but I could never take that step. I felt embarrassed and ashamed. I put off talking to anyone about my struggles for a long time. Socially and culturally, speaking to a therapist seemed almost heretical. To look for something other than a spiritual solution to the issues plaguing me created a crisis of faith. Meanwhile, the frustration with my compulsions and impure thoughts continued to mount. I was doing everything that I was asked to do by the Church, but nothing seemed to heal me from what was becoming an affliction in my mind. By 2017, I reached a breaking point. After years of suffering, I desperately wanted to be healed and finally decided to take the first big step and attended therapy.

I booked an appointment with Dr. Lonnie Stapp, a trauma therapist based in Coeur d'Alene, Idaho. He was a nice old man who was as wide as he was tall with a stylish haircut and a small soul patch under his bottom lip.

I didn't know what to expect. After several meetings, Dr. Stapp told me, "You might want to start writing down some notes because I think you will want to write a book about this." The next thing he said was, "We will have to revisit your childhood and your past."

I looked at him and said, "Hell no! I built a wall around that for a reason!" Then I walked out the door.

I had no interest in talking about my past—and I wasn't ready to. I found my past disgusting and believed there was no value in what had happened. The shame was real, and that extended to seeking help. It took me four weeks to tell Gina I was seeing a therapist. I drank an entire bottle of Gallo Santa Rita pinot noir during dinner before breaking the news to her.

Speaking about my childhood wasn't the only issue I had with Dr. Stapp. We also had very different philosophical and religious views about sexuality. My beliefs are deeply rooted in the principles of my Catholic faith. For example, the conjugal act, sexual intercourse, is a sacred collaboration between the husband, wife, and God to bring new life into the world. The great pleasure attached to these actions moves us to do these acts *and* take on the burden of caring for and educating the children that might be given to us. To separate the pleasure from the procreative end would be a grave evil. I realize this sentiment grates against modern sensibilities, yet change the context and it makes more sense. Few would praise the ancient Roman vomitorium, where the food consumed at a feast was deliberately vomited out so the person could continue to eat without discomfort.

I felt Dr. Stapp was trying to alter those beliefs. He wanted me to accept that it was okay for sex to be dirty; to accept that perhaps things like masturbation and pornography were okay in certain contexts. These were hard "no's" for me, and since we didn't have a common starting point, we made very little progress.

He proceeded to approach my situation from an addiction standpoint: *You're an addict, so let's explore how you became an addict and what you're going to do about being an addict.*

I have a difficult time associating what you do with what you are. Your actions are what you do, and I believe they are separate from what you are. We are all capable of doing things that we don't want to do, things we are not proud of. Do these actions define us? I don't believe there are many addicts who are proud that they are addicts. Most, if not all, fight to rid themselves of addiction, not use it to define them. By the time I had built up the courage to see Dr. Stapp, I already felt bad enough about myself. And I struggled with feelings of worthlessness. I didn't need to add addiction to my list of problems. After four months, I decided to stop working with Dr. Stapp, but I didn't give up on therapy altogether.

It's ironic that many elites and politicians still foster a culture of shame around therapy. At the same time, these people refuse to acknowledge the issues behind the fentanyl, heroin, and suicide epidemics afflicting our nation, which could be helped with the best therapeutic models we have now.

A friend of mine had recommended I see Mark Wilson, who referred to himself as a Christian relationship counselor. He had an extensive background in various pastoral ministries in different Protestant denominations, so I felt he would be a good fit. At least he wouldn't try to change my beliefs.

I started seeing him in 2017. Mark was different because he tried to affirm the goodness of my being and to help me reexamine my beliefs around my struggles, working hard to help me overcome shame and reach a place where I felt more comfortable being myself. I found these sessions to be beneficial.

Mark created a unique framework that helped me develop a sense of who I am, what I was designed to do, and the type of work would lead to the most fulfillment in life. He called it the Path Maker Psychometric Evaluation. It considers interests, abilities, and values (similar to StrengthsFinder), temperament (similar to Meyers-Briggs), and adds in consideration for organizational role and impact style. Through this system, I learned that I like creative roles and prototyping. I like to impact my environment through analysis and cooperation with others. I value risk, synthesis, strategy, and influence. I get my batteries recharged by solitude, analyze before allowing an emotion to land, and receive new information with a bias toward the future and possibility. I am flexible, always keeping options open, sometimes to a fault. Those insights have been very helpful when navigating my personal and professional challenges.

In 2020, I booked a one-on-one session with Michael d'Esterre, a licensed Catholic counselor who specialized in cognitive behavioral therapy (CBT). I knew him through a family connection and, much like Dr. Stapp, he encouraged me to dive into my past, but in a much healthier way.

It was a book he recommended, *Be Restored* by Bob Schuchts, that laid the groundwork for my breakthrough. Schuchts's book was about recognizing the wounds to our sexual identity and then restoring that sexual identity to its proper place. He walked the reader through each developmental phase of life, from early childhood development progressing through adulthood, to illustrate what each phase looks like when applied in a real-world setting. Each chapter of the book included a series of questions to help you examine the ways you may have been sexually damaged or led astray.

Reading *Be Restored* was heartrending because it required me to revisit my childhood. While that was the impasse I had reached with Dr. Stapp, this book broke through that stigma because the questions it posed weren't judgmental. They framed sexual sin, promiscuity, and other sexual issues as an injury that could be healed, not an evil to be ashamed about. Dr. Schuchts compared actions (influenced by our environment and past experiences) to the fruit of a tree. If your tree doesn't bear healthy fruit, you don't just pluck off the rotten fruit. You must work to heal the tree, and then you'll get healthier fruit. With the help of this book, Michael enabled me to recognize that I had been harmed and damaged, and we worked to restore who I was. He wasn't trying to label me or keep me stuck.

He was trying to help rebuild me. That allowed me to view my past in a different light. Instead of feeling shame, I felt hope.

I spent my Saturdays going into town for Mass and then headed to a local coffee shop to read that book. I brought along a notebook and wrote long-form responses to all the questions as a way to explore my past. I was brutally honest with myself, going into every excruciatingly painful detail to record everything I could remember on the page. It was intense, and there were moments when it felt like my heart was broken.

In the summer of 2021, I reached my breaking point after a session in the coffee shop and had to stop for the day. On the drive home, I called Gina to let her know that I was on my way back. I felt so much grief, not just over what had happened to me but what had happened as a result of these things—how it had impacted my relationships and the people in my life. I grieved how emotionally shut down I had become; how distant I was from those I loved with all my heart. I suddenly felt deeply broken and was desperate for a savior. Crying and overwhelmed with sorrow, I had to pull over in the NAPA Auto Parts parking lot on Fourth Street.

"Are you okay?" Gina asked, sounding concerned as I sobbed. "Do I need to send someone to come get you?"

I knew I couldn't break down, so I got myself together and regained my composure. Grieving was what my body and soul needed, yet I didn't want Gina to see that grief. Deep down, I was afraid that if she knew how wounded I was, she would reject me. So I didn't talk about it with her.

Two months later, after I had spent weeks journaling and exploring my past on the page, Michael asked if I would be willing to share what I wrote with him and to read it out loud. That was the last thing I wanted to do, but if therapy was going to be successful, my past would have to come out sometime. I might as well draw out the poison now.

I read him the whole thing, starting from my earliest childhood memories of being exposed to pornography and walking in on someone (probably my father) having sex, up until the present. As I progressed, my breathing grew shallow, and my voice quieted to a whisper. I felt shame and then I dissociated. As a practicing Catholic, I go to confession regularly, but reading this—speaking every shameful wound and deed out loud—was much more difficult because it was detailed and specific. In confession, the priest doesn't want specifics; they want you to summarize the big picture. What I read couldn't get more specific.

When I finished, he looked at me and said, "I just want you to know. You think you're responsible for a lot of this stuff, and based on what you've just told me, I don't believe that's true. I suspect a lot comes from this harm that you endured as a small child."

Michael explained that what I experienced wasn't voluntary and how exposure to pornography was a form of sexual abuse. That didn't mean that my father wanted it to happen, but he allowed it to happen. If a parent left the front door open and allowed a vicious dog to maul their child, they would be responsible. That was what was done to me with pornography; it chewed me up. And while it might be difficult to acknowledge, that was a form of sexual abuse.

Michael said to cut myself some slack. "You're not this evil person who God can't help. You just have some bad programming that you haven't yet figured out how to un-program."

Being met with compassion instead of judgment was a radical new experience for me. Until that point, those feelings were always met with condemnation and shame. That compassion Michael showed created the space required to have more compassion for myself.

Michael also gave me a book on gratitude. In it, there was a chapter on self-love and about acknowledging that you are lovable. I wasn't ready to admit that I was lovable, but that book challenged some of my fundamental beliefs.

For example, the Second Great Commandment is to "Love your neighbor as yourself." But if you don't love yourself, how can you be expected to love your neighbor? What does it mean to love yourself? For a long time, I had struggled to understand this until I asked one of the priests what it really meant. He told me to imagine how Jesus would treat me if He was standing right next to me. Since He embodies perfect love, that's how I should treat myself, but that's something we humans rarely do.

How often do we get lost in our thoughts and speak negatively to ourselves? Jesus would never say something harmful to us. He would never be verbally or emotionally abusive, yet we constantly give ourselves dressings-down. I had to decide to be better to myself, to avoid being harsh (such as by calling myself "stupid"), because I didn't deserve the harm it caused.

That required reading the chapter on self-love in that gratitude book several times before finally realizing that just because I thought something that didn't make it true. What was true was true, whether I thought or felt it. My beliefs didn't create truth. That was the nature of reality. Just because I was beating myself up and thinking that God didn't love me did not make it true. It didn't matter if I thought I was unlovable, because if I was loved by others and by God, then by definition I was lovable because that was true. God doesn't make bad things, so if He made me, I could not be bad. That realization changed the way I talked to myself, and it challenged me to reexamine my belief system.

I had a choice: I could remain prideful and stubborn by continuing to believe that I was not lovable, or I could learn to accept reality. That's the essence of humility—the acceptance of reality regardless of whether you think or feel something is true. Being able to reframe my thinking to focus not on my thoughts or feelings, but on what I knew to be true paved the way for me to actually think and feel those things.

I reached a point in 2023 where I felt that I had gotten all I could from Michael and the CBT approach. That's when I started seeing Nichole Salinas, a therapist who specialized in childhood trauma.

Nichole introduced me to EMDR—Eye Movement Desensitization and Reprocessing therapy. It is a form of therapy that involves focusing on a traumatic memory from your past while moving your eyes back and forth. That stimulation helps the brain process the painful memory and diminish its power. You essentially create new neuropathways that reprogram the brain.

She layered this approach with Internal Family Systems (IFS) therapy, based on the idea that we all have different parts within us, each with its own story and purpose. By understanding the nature of these parts, we can create a stronger relationship between the self and those parts.

Many people who experience childhood trauma become disconnected from their physical sensations and emotions. They grow accustomed to suppressing their feelings, and in a way, they become disassociated from their bodies. It takes a lot of work to recultivate that connection to sensation and emotion to feel fully human once again. EMDR and IFS proved to be effective ways for me regain that connection with a part of myself that I had suppressed for so long.

My first world-changing epiphany occurred while working with Michael d'Esterre. My work with Nichole enhanced that progress. By 2023, I had a much better understanding of how my past influenced my current struggles and that what I experienced wasn't my fault. That's when the next breakthrough occurred.

Our parents (especially our fathers) represent for us what God the Father could be like. They are the ones who introduce us to this concept of family. I realized that I had been seeking my father's approval all of my life, starting from when I was a child and continuing through adulthood. It's why I was so devastated when he said he didn't trust me. For most of my life, I had wanted him to say, "Yeah, you're good at this. Yeah, I trust you. Yeah, you've got this." It's not that he never encouraged me or told me he loved me, but those statements were not common, and that wasn't the message he communicated.

I've learned to let go of that need to be accepted or get approval from my father because I don't know if that will ever happen. But whose child am I really? Ultimately, our happiness depends on accepting not our father's love but God's love. I believe that true happiness can only be found through our union with God. Those who accept that love tend to be happier despite the suffering they may experience here on earth. However, there was a disconnect between what I learned in therapy and what I was being taught in the Church. Even though I had made significant breakthroughs, a part of me still questioned if I was truly living up to that moral code. That created a lot of turmoil.

I spoke with my pastor at Immaculate Conception and he took a hardcore approach that was not in alignment with what I had been told by my therapists. "You need to take psychotherapy and psychology with a grain of salt. Sometimes, those sciences drift into the pseudoscience territory, and we, as children of God, operate in the realm of the soul. Psychologists don't always have the answer."

It was clear he didn't even want to consider that there was a different way to think about this, instead viewing it as taking the easy path. Luckily, not every priest had the same staunch beliefs.

Father Benoit Philippon was a Frenchman who taught at Immaculate Conception Academy. He was only thirty, and at six two, he was wiry and athletic like a soccer player. Our first interaction occurred in the confessional in 2024. I told him what had been going on and what I had learned from different therapists. His reaction was much different from that of our pastor. He said, "Okay, well, if that's what they say, that makes sense to me."

I continued to speak with him in the confessional once a week. I shared what I had been reading and learning and asked for his help in better understanding what I was experiencing from the Church's perspective. He got to know me. He saw me in church and with my family around town. He knew what I struggled with were compulsions and not willful acts. Sin is a big deal. Nobody wants to offend

God, but he could see that I was clearly distressed about my predicament, so he treated me with compassion.

It wasn't only my therapists and priests who helped me heal. I also relied heavily on close friends for continued support. I'm still very good friends with my best man, Scott Wilson. I talk to him once a month, and we discuss very intimate things. He's been there for me to lean on throughout this therapeutic process. The same is true about my old roommate from Salt Lake City, Steve Brousard, who let me crash on the floor of his duplex. He holds me accountable by pointing out the mistakes I make and providing encouragement when I'm down. I would not be where I am today without the support from all of these different sources—each important in its unique way. Those conversations with friends are therapeutic. They bring us closer together and help to heal that trauma.

There is such pressure on us, socially and professionally, to adhere to a predetermined standard. And if you don't, it's easy to think that you're worthless or a bad person, but I no longer believe that. I know that I am not a bad person. I have my flaws, and I am not 100 percent responsible for the feelings, urges, and thoughts that filled me with shame when I was younger. I didn't bring that on myself. It wasn't my fault. I learned to accept that and to understand it was part of who I am. That realization and understanding have been life changing. Finally, I feel that I am in control. That's valuable. That's real power.

If any of this sounds familiar, you're not alone in this struggle. The shame you carry, the voice that tells you you're not enough, it doesn't define you. Just as I had to learn to separate my worth from the expectations of others, you too can question those harsh inner critics. What would it feel like to extend the same compassion to yourself that you would offer a friend? Everyone's journey toward self-acceptance is different, but it begins by understanding that you are not broken for having struggled. God is waiting for you to open your heart and soul to Him. Then, you'll have everything you need within you to reclaim your power. It just doesn't happen all at once.

Brillianteering is a term used to describe the final stage of diamond polishing. It's the process of taking a rough diamond and chipping away at it until you're left with a brilliant sparkling jewel. The jeweler doesn't sit there and chip away at the same spot repeatedly. They come at it from different angles until they're able to shape the diamond in a way that maximally reflects the light. I can't help but think of my therapeutic and spiritual development during these years the same way. There was no one person, approach, or modality that resulted in the progress that helped me reach the point where I am today. It was a long journey of having those rough edges chipped away from different angles before I could see the beauty of what was inside.

The process was painful, but it's what allowed me to make more progress than I ever thought possible when I first sat across from Dr. Stapp in 2017. What's interesting is that what he told me about the need to open up about my childhood was right. I resisted, but many of the issues I struggled with, and that continue to bubble up in my everyday life, can be traced directly back to my childhood.

It's taken a lot of work for me to discuss this openly. I've since learned how important that is to the healing process. It goes back to humility—knowing what's true, accepting it, and then acting from there. It doesn't mean it's always comfortable, but it's true, and that's what matters most.

Many people today try to downplay what has become known as little-"t" trauma, especially men. That tough-guy mentality prevents many from dealing with their emotions. As a society, I believe we should do the opposite and normalize emotional intelligence. You can't always pull yourself up by the bootstraps. And you can't sit there and wallow in your trauma or ignore it and expect it to go away on its own. You must take action, or else it will manifest in unexpected ways, especially when you don't understand the underlying cause.

There's a saying in the recovery world: "wounded people wound people." When people experience trauma early in life and fail to address it, they often become more likely to hurt those around them. It's not deliberate, but they pass it on, which is why we need to have compassion around this discussion of trauma instead of placing blame.

The much more productive approach is to ask why these problems have surfaced in adulthood. Another book that really helped was *What Happened to You?* by Bruce D. Perry and Oprah Winfrey. It discusses tracing trauma back to the root cause, which often lies in childhood experiences. The incredible stories told in that book helped me wrap my head around the long-term impacts of traumatic events from my past. The deeper I dug, the more sense it made.

Coming to that realization was an incredibly humbling experience, and I know I am not alone. Similar experiences have harmed many people, and they often don't understand that their problems today can be traced back to early childhood. Some of those experiences that people might not even remember have a lasting impact with far-reaching consequences. We're very hard on people for succumbing to addiction and other common trauma-related manifestations, but by not acknowledging and addressing the root cause of their issues, we're making it extremely difficult for them to improve their condition. Until you understand what's happening and why, it's difficult to change the neurological response patterns.

I've made tremendous progress since 2020, yet I still don't feel like that experience in the closet is ever truly behind me. I have to be careful because I know there's a possibility that I could return to that dark place again. I'm not as invulnerable and invincible as I once believed. You can fix a broken mug with superglue. Superglue is amazing, but some of the fractures held together by the glue can weaken over time and easily break off again.

I know that I need to maintain my support networks. My journey began with great therapists like Mark, Michael, and Nichole and extended to understanding priests like Father Philippon and Father Hawker. My relationships with my wife and children are vital connections that bring me tremendous joy. My relationship with my biological mom and my Aunt Nancy, as well as my sisters, Shawn and Causja, help to keep me grounded and balanced. I make sure to speak regularly with my friends and not shut them out. I need to stop looking for approval from places that aren't going to provide it. I've learned not to bottle up emotions, and I know that when painful emotions bubble up, I should not suppress them, because the sooner I acknowledge those emotions are present, the sooner they can be addressed. That's the work I must consistently do, and it unfolds one day at a time.

CHAPTER 13

The Process and the People

THE BREAKTHROUGHS I experienced in therapy were the first step, but that didn't mean everything magically fell into place. I needed to apply what I learned to my everyday life. As I emerged from my darkest period, I found myself approaching everything differently: my business, my faith, and my family. Nowhere was this shift more apparent than in how I began to understand what true success actually meant.

When I was getting Precision Precast Erectors off the ground, Jay Abraham told me how business was about the process and the people, not the result. I said I understood, and I thought I did, but it didn't sink in for me until 2021. The company had just earned $1 million in revenue a month. I was holding a check for $1 million in my hands. We had come so far from the days of seeking out hard-money loans to keep the company afloat. Even just a few years before, I never would have imagined that was possible. By all standard metrics, we were successful. But when I looked at that check, all I could think was, *"Wow, all of this is going to pay the bills."*

That's when I realized what Jay was trying to say. The results—at least the financial results—were not nearly as satisfying as I once thought they were. When bidding out a project or reviewing the books, it's easy to fall into that trap and become overly focused on the result. That's when I have to stop and remind myself that it's about the process and the people, because what am I really trying to do with this company? We build concrete boxes. So, if we succeed, great, another city has one more big ugly gray box. (To be fair, we do occasionally get to do stunning work, like the Ritz-Carlton in Portland.) That's why I've changed how I think about the company and its success, focusing instead on the people we impact.

I look at the growth of my brother-in-law Caleb Wohletz, who first started working for the company in 2013 as an apprentice doing caulking and then ironwork before he rose through the ranks to become our operations leader, which is like a COO on steroids. My general superintendent, Cory Dawson, has been a union ironworker for twenty-five years and is now our general superintendent. We worked with Shad McDaniel even before PPE when we were at Central Premix and have watched him grow with us to become a major leader. My younger brother, Jean Luc, with whom I shared a bedroom in our grandparents' house in California when he was only three years old, has now worked his way up through the company into a leadership role. It's not only the success of our employees that is satisfying; it's seeing how that success has helped them provide better lives for their families. That is the true reward for me as a business owner.

Instead of focusing on what I can get, a significant part of the process for me has been considering how I can give back. One way is to build up people and take a more holistic view of employees rather than viewing only their output on an hourly basis. It involves working closely with our leadership team on soft skills, which I refer to as human skills. It's teaching them how to have difficult conversations, how to cope with adversity, and how to present themselves. Some people assume that others should automatically show them respect. Others have chips on their shoulders because they believe people see them as just dirty blue-collar workers.

You take control of how others perceive you by dressing

appropriately. It may sound trivial, but many of the individuals who work for us don't realize the importance of a first impression and don't consider the one they give to others. If they pay more attention to their appearance on the jobsite, they can command more respect and change how people perceive them. I remember telling our field leadership, "When people walk on this jobsite, you are going to look so good and look like you are in charge that people are actually going to come to you instead of the general contractor's representative because they're going to think you're the one in charge."

To cultivate this, we made our annual Christmas party for our leadership team and core vendors a suit-and-tie affair. Many of our new leaders don't own a suit and tie, so they have to go out and buy one. Their spouses or girlfriends get excited because they get to buy party dresses and evening gowns. When they come together and see themselves wearing nice clothes, their self-image improves. That's just one way we've tried to take an interest in the human side of our employees, especially with the management and leadership teams.

I believe it's that people-and-process-first outlook that has helped the company grow. In 2022, we did $12.5 million in installation work. That figure increased to $17 million in 2023, and we matched it in 2024. We built the company up to forty full-time employees, and during our peak operating periods, we've had as many as 110 people total (part-time and full-time) on the books.

There has been a significant shift within the industry in recent years, as many innovative, high-horsepower thinkers and designers in leadership have walked away from the business due to a lack of available work. We first caught a glimpse of this after the crash of 2008–2009, and again in 2013. It gained further momentum during the COVID-19 pandemic in 2020. Some chose to retire, while others were forced out when companies downsized due to high salaries. This brain drain opened the door for the younger generation, and that's had mixed results.

Younger leaders are well-intentioned and have a lively spirit. They also tend to be tech-savvy and book-smart with construction management degrees. While that may help them understand the contractual side of the business, few are construction-smart. They lack the real-world jobsite experience. They don't understand how the sausage is made and often struggle to interact with those in the field, as they come from a different world. That can make business challenging at times.

By putting people first, we built a team of highly professional leaders. We knew they needed a home to finish out their careers, and we were happy to provide that for them. This emphasis on professionalism and leadership has saved us from many of the challenges our competitors face. That doesn't mean we don't have our challenges.

After pulling out of the buyout deal in 2021, my father continued to work. I had let him know that the buyout option was no longer on the table. He was full-time until 2023 when he experienced heart issues and needed to undergo a procedure to put a stent in his heart. There was the possibility that he would have to undergo open-heart surgery.

My father was in charge of sales when I told him, "If you need to undergo open-heart surgery, I'm going to hire someone to take over your department. And if you only need the stent, your priority when you return will be to hire and train your replacement."

Of course, he was upset and tried to argue, but I wasn't budging. As the person financially responsible for the company, I couldn't let my father's health issues put the long-term future of the company in jeopardy. And it's good we didn't wait to see how everything turned out, because he ended up needing triple bypass surgery. We immediately hired his replacement.

A month after his surgery, my father showed up at the office, trying to work. He was weaker and had been through an ordeal, but something else wasn't right. It was in the way he spoke and interacted—the things he said. He wasn't himself, and his mind wasn't as sharp. I learned that postoperative cognitive dysfunction was a potential side effect of open-heart surgery. I tried to sit him down and tell him that he needed to ease up and take a rest, but that went over like a lead balloon. He was going to do what he wanted to do, and that meant continuing to show up at the office, even if it was only for an hour or two. In a strange way, the move to hire his replacement earned his respect—even if he doesn't listen to or hear what I have to say.

This company is no longer about me or my father; it's about building something that lasts long after the concrete has crumbled to sand. When I look at what we've accomplished at PPE, I don't see buildings—I see the families we've helped support, the young men we've turned into leaders, and the proof that you can run a business without sacrificing your soul. That's the real return on investment.

The lessons Jay taught me about process and people weren't reserved for business. As I built PPE into something meaningful, I began to see that the same principle applied to every aspect of my life—including my relationship with God. You can't focus solely on the destination and expect to find peace along the way. Faith, like business, is about showing up every day and trusting the process, even when you can't see the final result. And much like business, my relationship with God is very much a process that has evolved through different phases.

The more you learn about yourself, the better you understand your weaknesses, and that reinforces the need for God to help you become the person you want to be—the person you were created to be. Everyone's relationship with God is an ongoing process. There is no endpoint where you reach peak holiness and alignment with God, except for death, which comes for us all. We all have faults and issues.

Over the years, I've become acutely aware of my need for a

savior, and that can result in overcompensation at times. In 2021, I was going through a difficult time and began attending Mass every day. I'd wake up at 4:15 in the morning, perform a quick meditation, dress, and be out the door so I could be at Mass at 5:45 a.m. I'd then do a light workout and hit the sauna to get myself mentally, physically, and spiritually prepared before starting the workday. It was a solid routine that was beneficial in many ways, but after doing that for two years, I had exhausted myself. My reserves were depleted before my day officially began.

My friend Scott had to remind me, "You're not obligated to do all of that. If you need to take some time away from this intense religious practice to get well, then that's what's best for you right now. You can't let it drain you and impact how you show up and perform your obligations."

There's the old story of a man who gave away all his money to charity to care for the poor and then was unable to feed his children at home. I was drifting in that direction, and Scott's advice hit close to home. I reevaluated my schedule and relationship with God to make them more closely aligned with what was truly important. It goes back to what Saint Thomas Aquinas said about not pursuing the inferior good.

Today, I don't put pressure on myself to attend Mass every day. Instead, every morning, I perform a thirty-minute Christian meditation that I learned at the monastery. It involves picturing God or using anecdotes from the gospel to form an image in your mind. I then direct my gaze up toward that image of God so I can have a conversation with Him. It requires quieting my mind to create space to hear the response. Much like any mindfulness meditation, it's not easy at first—it takes practice. The more you do it, the less you need to rely on the gospel, and you can eventually reach a point where you're in an ongoing conversation with God throughout the day as if it were second nature.

Developing a healthy relationship with God starts with understanding the minimum requirement and making sure I meet that.

I've got an app for that. Well, not literally, but I have developed a system to check in with myself about my spiritual well-being. According to the Church, I don't need to do much—attend Mass on Sunday, receive Communion, go to confession, and observe a little fasting during Lent. There's also a more subjective pulse check. I ask myself: Am I living a life of sin and breaking God's commandments, or am I living a life that's generally peaceful and joyful? Saint Paul discusses the fruits of the flesh versus the fruits of the Spirit. When you're not living and moving toward God, you're involved in foolishness, drunkenness, and fornication. When you're living in the Spirit, there's love and joy and peace and patience—qualities you can recognize in someone who seems to be living a good life.

And nowhere does it say that I have to do any of this alone. Anyone serious about growing in their spiritual life needs an adviser they can talk to and report to on their progress, allowing that person to take a more objective view and provide feedback.

It's not all about me. What's just as important is what I do for others.

I've been very lucky, and when you're blessed with treasure, you're not supposed to keep it for yourself. You're supposed to give back and use that treasure to make the lives of other people better. While I don't have infinite treasure by any means, I am more blessed than most. There is a lot of pain and suffering in the world, and if I have the means, I must lessen a portion of that if I can.

When Gina and I were first married, we promised to give 10 percent of our earnings to the Church and charity. It didn't matter if we were scraping by or not; it was always 10 percent off the top. That's easy to do when you're working for wages. A few years after we started the business, when we were actually generating a profit, things became complicated. Tithing isn't set up for cash flow. We had money on the books, but it wasn't all cash that I could spend. Some of that money was tied up in the company. At the end of 2012, Gina and I had to sit down and ask ourselves, "How much should we give? Do we give on the cash we received as if we were employees, or do we give based on the gross income?"

Gina then asked me, "Do you want to get blessed on the net or gross income?"

"The gross income."

"Then, we should probably give based on the gross income."

That made sense, so that's what we did. We scrimped and saved, pulling together what we had to make a donation based on our gross income. Sometimes, that's painful, but it's what we've always done.

I've lived in a monastery. I know that people devote their lives to serving God, the Church, and its members. In a religious order, they don't get a salary—they get a small stipend every month to buy their shampoo and deodorant and a few other minor things, but otherwise, they don't make money. They're not in it to make money. It's not a get-rich scheme. That, to me, is worth supporting.

There is also a significant amount of poverty and pain in the world. That's one of the reasons why we give to St. Labre Indian School, Food for the Poor, Wounded Warriors, and Paralyzed Veterans of America, to name a few. We also contribute to charity-focused funds at our church, where the funds are distributed to people in our community who are in need.

Once I adopted a healthier approach that allowed me to pursue the greater good more closely aligned with my life goals and obligations, I developed a deeper connection to God—a deeper reliance and trust—than at almost any other point in my life. My relationship with God will always evolve and is an ongoing process of self-discovery. That starts with understanding that we're not supposed to hoard our blessings—we're supposed to share them.

The hardest process to navigate has always been family. You can't just show up on Sundays and go to confession when it comes to the people who live under your roof or share your last name.

Family will test everything you think you know about forgiveness, patience, and love. It's where spiritual growth gets put through the wringer, especially when trying to break destructive cycles that go back generations.

I love my dad very much. I want him to be physically, mentally, and spiritually healthy. I'm happy to see the progress he's made growing in his humanity and love for God. I believe that he is a much better man today than he was when I was younger. I want to see him when I get to heaven. However, our relationship has always been complicated, and I don't think we will ever become super close, but I have reached a place where I can forgive him.

I believe that forgiveness, forgetting, and pain are interconnected. Forgiveness does not mean that you will forget. In fact, trying to forget or repress painful feelings can result in serious psychological consequences that often lead to addiction, promiscuity, and isolation. Forgiveness also doesn't mean that the pain will go away. It means that you're releasing the debt that's owed to you. You can choose whether you want to reconcile, but that's separate from letting go of the debt owed. I haven't forgotten what happened, and there is still pain, but I've let go of the debt. I'm done looking for justice. That's forgiveness.

At times, it almost feels like I have two families, and it has been in our best interest to maintain a certain distance between them. Gina and I, along with our boys, have made a concerted effort to prioritize our "little" family. We don't feel obligated to attend every function put on by every sibling and cousin. We can't go to every birthday party or extended-family gathering where all my siblings will be in attendance. Some of them get a little upset by that. But given the size of our extended families, it's just not practical. We'd have no time to do anything else. So, we do our own thing for our kids and don't impose it on the extended family. We're just going to be our family. It allowed us to create a healthy level of separation between us and the dysfunction in my extended family.

Trying to be home more often and spending time with my

family has been a continuous process, but the nature of my work has always kept me on the road. That can be difficult, but it makes those times when I am around the family even more special. I love sitting around the kitchen table to have a good meal with Gina and the kids. I love listening to their stories and hearing them laugh. That brings me a lot of joy, and home-cooked meals are always better than eating on the road.

Pretty much every night when I'm home, we all sit down together for dinner. I can think of only a handful of times where we've said, "Hey, we're going to go have pizza and watch a movie while we eat." That's very rare.

During the COVID-19 pandemic, I purchased sailing lessons with a local instructor for my family. Idaho was much more lenient with COVID-19 restrictions, and you could actually get out and do things. We all had a great time, and that inspired me to buy a small Hobie Getaway sailing boat. Over the years, we've spent quite a bit of time on that little boat cruising around Lake Coeur d'Alene and Heyburn Lake.

The best way I've discovered to spend quality time with the kids is through lacrosse. Immaculate Conception Academy dropped their rugby program in 2021 and tried to stir up interest in lacrosse as a replacement spring sport. Don Gary, a good friend of mine who had played lacrosse at the University of Maryland, was voluntold to be the head coach, and I wanted to help him out. That's how I learned about the sport, and it's what got my kids interested. Now all six sons have played. Over the past four years, we've extended the program from high school to include middle school teams, and now the program is open to fifth graders. Today, we have over eighty kids in the program. I feel honored to play a role in developing these young men and try to teach some of the life lessons that I believe have made me successful.

Life is good, but it's not always easy. Marriage is another process with its ups and downs, but that has always been part of the deal. Sometimes we each need our space, and as difficult as those times can be, there is some good that comes from it. It's spurred me to do a lot of the work that helped me become a better man. It goes back to everything happening *for* me and not *to* me.

I love my wife deeply, and I know she loves me just as much. During one of our most difficult times, when we weren't communicating as well as we could, she would pack a lunch for me in a brown paper bag every day and draw a smiley face on it. That was her way of telling me she still loved me. Today, I have an entire box full of paper bags with smiley faces on them to remind me of that love. That gives me strength when times are difficult.

I've always been someone who stepped outside my comfort zone and into new endeavors: sailing, motorcycle riding, woodworking, coaching lacrosse. I'm not afraid of adventure, of putting myself out there and pushing boundaries. As I write this, I'm doing it with golf, challenging myself right down to the clubs I've chosen to play with.

I don't want to make things easier. I want to identify where my game is weak so I can improve faster.

While singing in the Immaculate Concept Schola during Holy Week back in 2002, I found myself thrust into an uncomfortable position. During the Tenebrae service, we were singing Matins and Lauds—those beautiful, haunting morning offices that took hours to complete. Each member of the Schola had been assigned specific readings to chant using the traditional tones and melodies we'd practiced carefully beforehand.

As we reached one particular reading, nobody stepped forward. There was nothing but dead air. Whoever had been assigned it had simply forgotten. The silence stretched uncomfortably as I realized someone needed to fill the gap. Without preparation, without having mapped out where my notes would fall, I stepped up to the lectern. My heart pounded as adrenaline surged through me, and I began chanting the reading. To my horror, I started too high—in what felt like soprano range—which forced me to sing the entire passage in falsetto, my face burning tomato-red with embarrassment. But I finished it. I stepped in to fill a need, even if it meant singing higher than I'd ever sung in my life. It wasn't comfortable, but sometimes filling the gap isn't about comfort—it's about doing what needs to be done.

Sometimes that process leads me to places I never expected to go, and sometimes filling the gap means stepping into an arena I never thought I'd enter. There is no bigger challenge—no greater example—of stepping outside my comfort zone than deciding to run for the US Senate in 2026. While I am well-suited for office, I am unprepared for the deception and plotting that makes up the dark side of politics. I'm not ready for people to wine and dine me, to get me to sponsor something, with who knows what kind of influence offered behind the scenes. I am not looking forward to that part of the process.

I'm doing it because someone needs to step up to fill a need.

CONCLUSION

The Emperor's New Clothes

IN FEBRUARY 2025, I had breakfast with my friend Congressman Russ Fulcher. He was in town for the Lincoln Day dinner, which is hosted by the county Republican Central Committees to raise funds and awareness about candidates and issues. Over breakfast, I confided my plans to run for the US Senate. We discussed the campaign prospects and potential pitfalls. Russ was supportive; we brainstormed ideas and he agreed to help if he could. When Idaho's incumbent senator, James Risch, reached out to Russ to serve as chairman of his reelection committee, he had to decline the offer as it would have created a conflict of interest. Even though Russ has helped Risch in the past, he didn't want to damage our friendship. He explained to the senator that he was planning to help me with my campaign. When the senator heard that, he invited me to DC to meet with him in person at his office.

When I received the invitation, I prayed about it for a few days. After speaking with Justin Matheson, my senior campaign strategist, we decided that it would be beneficial to meet. It's not an uncommon request for the incumbent senator to meet with his challenger. Besides, I was curious to hear what he had to say. Since I would already be on the East Coast for a Boston conference in May

2025, I agreed to fly down to DC afterward. It would be a quick trip. I'd arrive in the morning and fly back to Boston that evening.

I had visited Washington, DC, multiple times and had brought a few of my sons with me on those trips. I had been mulling a potential Senate run since 2008, so I figured I should get a feel for the area. On one of those trips, one of Congressman Fulcher's interns gave us a tour of the US Capitol Building. Russ and I have met several times over breakfast at the Republican Club—the place where elected officials meet donors and friends (there are restrictions on whom they can see and what they can discuss in their state-funded offices). We've prayed together there, talked about family, spiritual healing, and theology. And, of course, some politics.

My trip to DC in May 2025 to meet with my political opponent, Senator Risch, was my first time in the Russell Senate Office Building. It was imposing by design—the high ceilings, ornate furniture, and sheer square footage were all meant to convey power and authority. I was waiting in the reception area, admiring the art on the walls, when I felt a hand clap me on the back. I turned around to see my friend, Russ.

"Do you mind if I join?" he asked.

"Of course not," I said. "I wondered if you might come by."

Shortly thereafter, we were escorted into the senator's office, which was three times the size of Russ's. A large fireplace dominated the center of a room filled with opulent decor meant to exude power. Even with the Federal-period-style furniture and giant mahogany desk, the office could still easily fit thirty or forty people.

Senator Risch was a small, yet surprisingly trim man who was eighty-two. Having served as an elected official at the state and federal level for more than fifty years, he wore the DC uniform well: gray suit, white shirt, and red and blue striped tie with polished black oxfords.

As Russ and I sat in the chairs across from the senator, he handed us a photo printed on a piece of copier paper. "What do you think of this?" he asked.

I looked at the picture of the senator talking to President Trump in the Oval Office.

When I handed back the photo, he said, "Trump has my back, and he listens to me."

Then he asked, "Why are you running for Senate?"

"God had put it in my heart seventeen years ago," I said. "And after many years of remote preparations, He, through an intermediary, told me that He wanted me to run now." Had I a picture of myself with my God, I'd have shown it to him then.

"God wants me to run, too," the senator said. "Do what you want, but I'm not leaving, and I don't lose campaigns. Period. This is *my* seat. I'm the seventeenth person to ever hold this seat."

The conversation turned to local Idaho politics until the senator received a call to make a procedural vote on the Senate floor. He invited me to join him.

What many people don't realize is that Capitol Hill has a myriad of tunnels beneath it, so that congresspeople, senators, and staffers can travel unmolested via tram from the Capitol to their offices. I hopped on a tram with the senator and his chief of staff, Ryan, to the Capitol Building, where we took an elevator up to the Senate floor. Ryan and I waited outside the door among the media, who were interviewing senators whom I had seen during countless TV spots. I'd be lying if I said I wasn't awestruck by the hubbub.

A few moments later, Senator Risch emerged from the Senate floor and whistled—whistled!—at us to follow him back the way we came. I was incensed that he would treat *anyone* that way. We shared the elevator down to the tram with Senator Tom Cotton of Arkansas, but I kept my excitement in check.

When we were back in the senator's office, he played a voicemail from President Trump, wishing him well. Afterward, I asked if giving him a small gift would break any Senate rules. He told me it didn't, so I presented him with a one-ounce silver coin pressed with an image of the Sacred Heart of Jesus. He didn't seem to recognize the image, which surprised me. *Isn't he also a Catholic?* And he'd just claimed to receive direction from God to run again.

On my way out the door, I asked, "What am I not asking that you think I should?" I thought there might be some key issue for Idaho that we hadn't yet discussed. Nope. He beat the same old drum.

"If Trump is really in my corner. And he is! He'll come stump for me in Idaho whenever I ask him to."

What struck me about our meeting wasn't what he said—it was the attitude that permeated the conversation, the entire building. There was a sense of entitlement, a feeling that those seats *belonged* to certain individuals by virtue of their experience, connections, and wealth. It whispered, "I deserve to be here. This is *my* seat."

No elected official "deserves" to be in office. That seat doesn't belong to anyone, no matter how much time they've put into the job of US senator, no matter how many favors they've accumulated, and no matter how much money they have. The people elect you to serve as their representative and act on their behalf. That's what grants you the opportunity to be a senator—not your experience, not your political pedigree, and certainly not your sense of entitlement. The idea of being entitled to a seat in government borders on aristocracy.

That is not who we are as a country.

The trip was beneficial in a significant way. The shock and awe factor had been blunted, if not disappeared entirely. Any intimidation I might have felt, any sense that I didn't belong in that world, was gone. I've been there. I've seen it. Politicians are normal people, flesh and blood, just like me. By the time I returned home, my purpose had been refined and my decision to run reinforced.

Pursuing politics or any position of power can be highly corrosive, and it's no secret that corruption is a persistent problem. When it comes to party politics, elected officials are expected and pressured to fall in line, to be a team player by doing what's best for the party and the institutions, not necessarily the people or their values. People with similar biases form coalitions to create echo chambers that grow impervious to outside opinion or change. Spend enough time in that system and it becomes increasingly difficult to think about issues in a different way. That's what has happened in DC.

We all have biases. That's part of the human condition. But it takes someone from outside the system to resist the corrosion. I haven't lived in the DC world. I didn't make my bones "playing the game." I took the "dirty hands, clean money" route instead. I believe that helps me to approach the issues of the day with an eye toward innovation and solutions that benefit the common good. I've been impacted by the same issues as the people in my community, so I understand their importance. Issues like fiscal responsibility, political accountability, appointing impartial judges, being able to earn a living wage, the widespread private ownership of capital, and the cost of health care. When my opinion doesn't line up along party lines, I can step out of the crowd to say, "Look, the emperor isn't wearing any clothes."

It's not about doing what's comfortable or fitting in with the party; it's about filling a need while remaining true to your values—an approach I try to practice every day.

When I sit down for a meal, whether I'm at home with Gina and the kids or having breakfast with Congressman Fulcher in the Republican Club, I say a blessing before the meal. That sounds like a small thing, but consider how few people say a blessing in public anymore. Even if they pray at home, there's something about being in public that makes people feel they're not allowed to do this. That's the same pressure that exists in Washington—to conform, blend in, and not rock the boat.

It will be critical to maintain a life of prayer in that environment. The pressures in Washington are real, and the temptations to compromise your values for the sake of political expediency are constant. I've seen what that system can do to good people. And I always have my golf game to keep me humble. Every time I step onto that course, the game reminds me that I'm not as good as I think I am. That's a lesson I'll remember every day in the Senate. Recognizing and admitting those flaws are what will keep me humble. And humility will be essential if I'm going to resist the corrupting influences of power and stay true to the people who sent me there.

I'm not the only one who sees a need that must be filled. It's obvious to many in the community. Many of those dissatisfied people understand parliamentary procedure and how to play the political game better than I do. Many have the political acumen to do a good job, but they haven't stepped up because they don't want to risk it or it's not in line with their self-interest. As a result, nobody accepts responsibility and the toxic cycle—the lack of effectiveness, leadership, and initiative—continue. Someone needs to step up and work for the people who are overlooked by our elected officials to promote once again the common good.

I want to give people hope. Hope that our political figures can still devise innovative solutions to our most difficult challenges rather than settling for inadequate compromises. Hope that, on a simpler level, good and decent people can still make a positive difference and get us out of the rut we are in. Serving as a beacon of that hope would make this experience worthwhile.

The decision to run for office wasn't an easy one to make and I didn't take it lightly. The commitment will impact my entire family. When we sat down for a big family meeting in January 2025, my eighteen-year-old son Malachi said, "It kind of makes me sad that you're going to run for office because that means you will be gone again. I'm graduating from high school, and I was looking forward to having more time to do things with you. But I still want you to run for Senate, Dad. The country needs you."

That hurt yet also made me incredibly proud. I know all my sons love me very much. I think they also wished that I was more like other dads—working a nine-to-five and coming home to mow the lawn and grill burgers on weekends. But sometimes doing what's right requires sacrifice, not just from the person making the decision, but from the whole family.

When I'm traveling for the campaign, when I miss those family dinners around our kitchen table that bring me so much joy, when I can't hear their stories and laughter, I remember what I'm fighting for. I'm fighting for a country where my sons' generation won't have to accept a poor compromise as the best we can do. I'm fighting for a system where everyday people can make a difference. I'm fighting to prove that politics isn't reserved for those who worship power.

People gave Jimmy Carter a hard time. Yet Carter was actually one of the few politicians not driven by power. He didn't want a career in politics. He grew up on a peanut farm in a mixed community in Jim Crow, Georgia, at a time when white kids didn't play with black kids. But Carter did because he hadn't been programmed not to yet. He attended the Naval Academy and served in the Navy before deciding to run for governor of Georgia, as he felt there were no other candidates worth voting for. That attitude of stepping up to fulfill a need took him all the way to the White House. That same attitude of stepping up to serve moved George Washington, Theodore Roosevelt, Ronald Reagan, and Donald Trump. That's the tradition I'm part of—leaders who step forward not because they want power, not because they want more money, and not because they belong to a certain party. They saw a need and were willing to serve.

In our current system, power flows from corporations to Washington in the form of money, drowning out the people's power. The Washington establishment I encountered on that DC trip in May has forgotten something fundamental: in America, power is supposed to flow from the people upward, not from the institutions downward. That Senate seat doesn't belong to anyone except the citizens of Idaho who choose someone to loan it to for six years.

I'm asking for that seat. Not because I deserve it and not because it's my turn, but because I can serve that seat with integrity, fight for innovative solutions, and prove I can make a difference in our democracy.

The shock and awe of Washington has worn off. I've seen behind the curtain, walked those marble halls, sat in those imposing offices. What I found wasn't intimidating—it was disappointing. These aren't titans of democracy; they're people just like me and you who've forgotten where they came from and started believing their own press.

The emperor is wearing no clothes. And it's time someone dares to say so.

Acknowledgments

FIRST, I would like to thank my wife, Gina. Through all the joys and sufferings of a beautiful marriage, you have patiently borne the trials of accompanying me on my journey. You truly have brought out the best in me. Next, my sons, who have inspired me to be a better man, a better father, and better husband. I hope you'll forgive me for my failures and pray for my final perseverance.

I also want to thank my dad—far from perfect, and yet just what God knew I needed to become the man He wanted me to be. To my mom, you've always been my biggest cheerleader, and I appreciate you. To Maria, thank you for all the love. You did your best and no one can ask for more. To my brothers and sisters, especially Shawn, Causja, and Jean-Luc, thank you for your love and your ears. I appreciate you. A special hug for my Aunt Nancy, a place of refuge.

Thank you to my brother and sister Ironworkers, who have been there for me my whole life. Thank you to all the priests and brothers who have aided me and taught me to be a better man and better Catholic. Special thanks to Fr. Hawker, may you rest in peace, and Fr. Beck, Fr. Phillipon, and Père Albert, OP.

To my friend Russ Fulcher, I thank you for your kind friendship and support. I deeply value our conversations over the years and look forward to working with you to make America and Idaho greater than ever. To my friends John Green, Tony Wisniewski, Dr. Peter Chojnowski, Hendrik Mills, Jake Eberlein, and Michael McGowan, your support and trust to let a blue-collar guy like me soar with eagles like you changed my life. And to my best friends,

Scott Wilson and Steve Broussard, you've been life savers to me over the years. You are the older brothers I never had.

Special thanks to all the highly trained professionals that helped me repair the damage from a lifetime of riding hard and putting myself away wet—in no particular order, Dr. Lonnie Stapp, Mark Wilson, Michael D'Esterre, Nichole Salinas, and many others. To my dear friends in the BIGS mastermind and the Helix mastermind, thank you for your help and encouragement over the years.

Thank you to my team at KAA. Executive Editor Stephen Power, you asked decidedly astute and acute questions and always kept us focused on the goal. Senior Editor Sabrina Young, you brought great insight into the book, and you (rightly) recognized what a badass my wife is. Lee Moreau, you kept us on track—and for a creative like me, that's invaluable. And Ryan Dempsey, my writing partner: you arguably now know more than any other human about my life. The delicacy and compassion you showed in this process meant the world to me.

Thank you to Michael and the team at Skyhorse Publishing. You held our toes to the fire and helped us deliver an exceptional manuscript on time. The work your team did on the cover and copy went beyond my expectations.

To all those whom I have neglected to thank, you are not forgotten. At mass, I always add "and all those I ought to be praying for" at the end of the Prayers for the Living. God knows who you are, and you will be rewarded for your charity towards me.

Oh, and Ms. Jeannette LaFors and Mrs. Karen P. Minor, your history classes changed my life and my writing forever!

About the Author

Denny LaVé is a man shaped by hardship, faith, and grit. Born into chaos in 1976 and raised amid instability, he survived a childhood marked by trauma, dislocation, and neglect that would break most. Yet through it all, he held on to a quiet conviction that life could be different.

As a young man, Denny joined the Marine Corps, experienced a near-fatal heatstroke, and later spent nearly two years as a Dominican novice in a monastery. He worked as a high-rise ironworker, scaling towers and riding the rails of America's blue-collar working class. Eventually, he cofounded Precision Precast Erectors, leading it to five consecutive Inc. 5000 awards before stepping aside to mentor others and prepare for a deeper calling.

Denny's journey spans spiritual exploration, business success, emotional healing, and political awakening. He has been recognized by the Idaho Department of Labor, and featured in the *USA Today*, *Forbes*, and *Construction Today*. Today, he lives in North Idaho with his wife Gina and their six sons. He is an active member of the Catholic Church, coaches lacrosse, sails, swings a golf club, and grills grass-fed steak with gratitude.

This memoir is the story of a man forged in fire, standing up not just to survive but to lead, serve, and heal.